SECOND EDITION

COMMUNICATING IN ORGANIZATIONS

A Casebook

Gary L. Peterson, Editor
University of Puget Sound

Allyn and Bacon
Boston • London • Toronto • Sydney • Tokyo • Singapore

Series Editor: Karon Bowers
Editorial Assistant: Scout Reilly
Marketing Manager: Jackie Aaron
Editorial-Production Service: Matrix Productions Inc.
Composition and Prepress Buyer: Linda Cox
Manufacturing Buyer: Megan Cochran
Cover Administrator: Jenny Hart
Electronic Composition: Omegatype Typography, Inc.

Library of Congress Cataloging-in-Publication Data

Communicating in organizations : a casebook / Gary L. Peterson,
    editor. — 2nd ed.
      p.   cm.
    ISBN 0-205-29589-4
    1. Communication in organizations—Case studies.
    2. Organizational effectiveness—Case studies.   I. Peterson, Gary
L., 1935– .
HD30.3.C635   1999
658.4'5—dc21   99-29088
                                                           CIP

Printed in the United States of America

10 9 8 7 6 5 4 3 2   04 03 02 01 00

Contents

SECTION 2: *Managing Information Flow*   *51*

SECTION 3: *Understanding Interpersonal Roles and Relationships*   *67*

SECTION 4: *Recognizing Leadership and Management Styles*   *89*

SECTION 5: *Building Group and Team Effectiveness*   *111*

*All proper names within this case, including that of the author, have been changed to protect individual identities.

Preface

In the few years since the publication of the first edition of this casebook, many things related to organizational communication have been occurring—in organizations themselves, in theories or approaches to studying organizations, and in a proliferation of information about what has been happening. In those short years, organizational communication textbooks increasingly have offered cases as part of their coverage of the principles of the discipline. Textbook author friends and colleagues remarked to me some time ago that their publisher said they needed to have cases now to compete in the organizational communication textbook field. That and similar comments have provided a measure of confirmation for this case user, who insisted a dozen years ago that there was a need and a market for case studies in the discipline.

Of course, a wide selection of textbooks is available, something to appeal to instructors who vary in approach, needs, and levels of treatment. The degree and reach of theoretical coverage vary perhaps more than ever. Whatever the orientation of the textbook or authors, however, a value still remains to having at hand a selection of cases wherein students can observe at least segments of those principles examined. Whether the text author or the course instructor wishes to emphasize traditional functionalist, interpretivist, or critical perspectives, most cases carry incidents that can be examined from each or any of those views.

The publication of this revised casebook is a further effort to provide application materials that can complement a broad treatment of organizational communication issues and principles. The primary function continues to be to present slices of organizational life and events based on actual incidents of communication events.

The cases selected for this volume represent a combination of cases from the first edition that course instructors have indicated to be most useful, plus a set of new narratives that look more extensively at some of the areas deemed most illustrative of contemporary organizational issues. It is to this latter end that I have added a section on managing communication crises and have given additional treatment to the section on managing differences and diversity. There are still likely cases in one of the casebook sections that an individual instructor will use in a way that seems at odds with section headings. I personally hope that does happen frequently, for that is the way I tend to "read into" most cases—the ones in this compilation as well as others.

I remind readers—students and instructors alike—to remember that these case narratives or descriptions are from actual organizations, and although many are disguised, they have still had to undergo clearance for use as a published case. That means fidelity to whatever it was that occurred and what might have been said, without violating trust and confidentiality of those individuals who were the principals actually involved. The materials, the data, the incidents, the situations, and the characters, however, are all reality based; they are not fictionalized. Some case data are taken extensively from public print and electronic sources—the latter an increasingly valuable repository of information useful in case studies. Readers might be frustrated over the absence of all the details about the situation or organization. I have opted in this revision, as in the first edition, to present communication examples in condensed settings. Still, the reader will find in this edition fewer total cases and more that include somewhat more detail.

Structure and Arrangement of the Casebook

The Introduction about case study approaches for students has been retained, albeit shortened somewhat. Course participants should continue to expect their instructor will select from the range of cases and will likely skip about within sections as well as within the entire casebook. Cases are presented with a sample of questions that instructors may or may not choose to use as aids to analyzing and discussing that particular case. Additional recommended readings are included in the casebook with this edition, and not for the instructor only in the available Instructor's Manual. Cases are presented without analysis. The Instructor's Manual provides additional teaching notes and instructional suggestions to the course director for dealing with the case. Likewise, where additional postcase information about the situation is known, that too is in the guide.

Acknowledgments

I have tried to bring to bear additional insight gained through valuable interactions with experienced case researchers, writers, and users who are members of the World Association for Case Method Research and Application (WACRA). My interactions with those professionals in spectacular conferences in Switzerland, Scotland, and France have broadened my knowledge and understanding, my insight into the case-writing process, and my appreciation for the nature of learning through the use of cases.

I continue to marvel at the willingness and patience of case contributors to bear with me through changes of publisher, health challenges, and periods of indecision about getting this volume into print. Some of these cases were truly collaborations; others I have most happily scanned or copied into a master manuscript relatively unaltered from the author's experience and insight.

I am deeply grateful not only for the encouragement of colleagues who sent material to consider and get into print but also for the criticism and feedback I have received from those who have used the first edition—students and instructors alike. I extend appreciation to Karon Bowers at Allyn and Bacon for her patience and prompt responses to my e-mailed pleas for answers to questions and to the Allyn and Bacon production staff for their persistence and professional insight. I also wish to thank the reviewers of this edition: Stephen F. Nielsen, University of Nevada–Las Vegas; and Donald Treadwell, Westfield State College. I am especially indebted to my wife, Una Jean, who really does wonder whether retirement is but "virtual reality," as time or event.

Gary L. Peterson
Tacoma, Washington 1999

Introduction
Student Use of the Case Method

THE COMMUNICATION CASES IN THIS BOOK

Those who teach and publish in the organizational communication sphere of communication and business disciplines have made a case for case method as a primary instructional tool. Although many organizational communication textbooks now include cases to accompany chapter materials, there is a wide range in the length and comprehensiveness in those cases. This compilation of cases is a further effort to collect a significant number of situations with enough detail to warrant application of case analysis rigor—and be flexible enough to be used with a variety of textbooks.

An element of academic instruction shared by organizational communication education has been that instructors frequently seem to perpetuate the learning model in which instructor is source and student is receiver. Even a cursory reading of virtually any material about case studies will demonstrate that case method learning shifts responsibility sharply toward the student as an involved participant in a realistic situation. That means considerably more responsibility will rest with the classroom/seminar participant to have read thoroughly, to have prepared well—in advance—and be willing to accept full partnership in his or her own learning.

In upper-level and graduate business management and policy fields, it is not uncommon to encounter casebooks whose average case length runs about twenty-five printed pages. Such a lengthy case has not been the model of use here, where there are typically five- to seven-page cases.

Some are shorter; a few longer. The philosophy guiding this decision has been based on the experience of finding that briefer cases still are sufficiently detailed, realistic, challenging, and involving for the participants. Leenders and Erskine (1973) counsel that it is often "more important that a case be a useful teaching device than having all the information or too much realism" (p. 114). Furthermore, the same writers discuss trends of case length and quote "Ernie," an experienced case instructor: "with a short case you get better participation, whereas with today's longer, complex cases students fear being tripped up by the instructor and shun discussion" (p. 114).

The goal for this casebook is to offer cases as useful teaching devices: relatively brief, clearly presented, with sufficient detail and challenge to allow or demand careful case analysis and discussion. Cases generally attempt to do the following: (1) describe one or more events, in the present, usually in third-person perspective; (2) provide some organizational background, environment, commentary, or exhibits; (3) include available and pertinent firsthand data; (4) include a record of what people say and think; (5) develop a decision-making situation, with responsibility for a decision to be made by the reader (or by a key character in the case); and (6) place the whole into clear and readable narrative (Bennett & Chakravarthy, 1978; Champion & Bridges, 1969; Leenders & Erskine, 1973, p. 45).

One characteristic of the cases selected for this book is that the events portrayed frequently represent commonplace or ordinary happenings; that is, case writers have avoided focusing only on company-threatening, crisis situations. The need for a decision to be made or for some action to be taken, however, is still obvious. In cases in which a decision does not remain to be made, there is an opportunity to analyze or critique recent events. The commonplace nature of the situations may be their greatest value in the long run. These are the types of communication difficulties that managers and organizations report—events and situations that apparently recur with such frequency that understanding the causes and handling the problems require careful review and analysis.

A second characteristic of most cases is that a single incident may exemplify several aspects of organizational life and communication behavior. You should follow your instructor's lead regarding the focus of the case. Be prepared to identify and discuss other implications as you see them. Because one or more communication concepts can be embodied in a single case, your instructor might choose to use a particular case for a purpose other than that suggested in the text or section title. Be flexible in the way the cases are applied in a course or seminar outline. Your instructor might also wish to skip around in assigning cases from the casebook. Some cases will be more useful for the instructor's purposes, whereas others might not be used at all.

Remember, you will not be exposed to perfect or complete representations. Get used to the frustrations of incomplete information. Prepare to identify and deal with assumptions, inferences, deductions, and probabilities. You truly will learn more by sensing the gaps in information, raising the questions that still need answers, and then making qualified decisions than if you had all the data and could quantifiably justify every step and every choice. In most of the cases the actual organization and characters have been disguised. Be assured that disguising does not mean that the case or situation has been manufactured. Events and characters are either real or based on actual characters in the organization. We have attempted to provide case materials from a variety of organizations, including public and private agencies, traditional manufacturing or high-technology companies, small entrepreneurial ventures, and service organizations.

The questions that accompany each case should be used as a beginning point. Your instructor might assign them specifically or choose to ignore them in favor of another set of selected goals. Ideally, the questions will help you probe for specific data from the case, examine assumptions, and determine relationships to the principles or concepts discussed in the course or seminar (Weilbacher, 1970). Similarly, your instructor might choose to assign readings from the selected bibliography included at the end of each case or prefer to rely on text or other coverage of course principles.

USING THE CASE METHOD

This section provides recommendations for students or trainee participants who will be using the book. These suggestions should also prove valuable for other courses or training seminars in which the case method plays a prominent role in the instruction. Serious case study students are encouraged to read the student-oriented sections of the references cited here.

Practical suggestions for case use are provided in this introductory chapter, divided into four sections as follows:

- Purposes and Values of the Case Study Method
- Case Analysis Preparation

  - Examining for Case Facts
  - Examining for Problem and Solutions

- Demonstrating Case Analysis
  - Preparing Your Analysis
  - Preparing to Discuss
- General Suggestions for Case Participation

Purposes and Values of the Case Study Method

It might be worthwhile for the consumers of case studies—the students or participants—to understand what their instructors and learning theorists promote as the rationale for engaging in the case study method. The case approach is viewed as an excellent way for persons relatively inexperienced in organizational life and for those who need additional insight to develop a series of much needed skills.

First, case study work can help you identify principles and theories present in an actual situation. This experience comes from being thoroughly versed in what happened. As an observer, you see what went well or what went wrong. If a fault or problem is identifiable, you can connect reasons or causes based on mastery of theories or concepts. This ability can be fully realized only if you are thoroughly grounded in the principles covered by a text, other source materials, or direct experience and you transfer that understanding to the contexts of a case situation.

Second, experience with the case method builds needed analytical skills. Even in an extended case the focus tends to be narrow. As observer and analyzer, you have the benefit of giving special thought and cultivation to your diagnostic abilities. Remember, factual information might be easy to find, but answers or reasons typically are not stated in the case problem and must be searched out.

A third needed skill is the testing of problem-solving abilities through posing solutions and recommendations. Most cases end with problems unresolved, with difficulties remaining. The case student might then be asked not only to suggest how the immediate difficulties can be straightened out but also to pose solutions and justify the proposed recommendation(s).

Another important developmental skill involves learning to learn from peers. Many case method analysis sessions involve preparation and review in groups or teams. Even when discussion and analysis are conducted with an entire class, the individual case analyst invariably learns that others have perceptions and insights not seen in her or his own personal study. Because so much of work life in organizations revolves around teamwork, it is well to develop positive attitudes and success experiences about the contributions others can make.

Likewise, it is important to develop skill in articulating one's own insights and conclusions. Case instructors expect their students not only to carefully examine and understand the case situation but also to voice their insights, judgments, or recommendations. Sometimes the vocalization can be planned and presented formally; more typically the utterances will be impromptu. Clarity of expression is a highly valued ability in the case classroom and in life outside the classroom.

In addition to a willingness to speak out and to express opinions or conclusions, the case student learns—sometimes dramatically—how to defend and support personal and independent judgments. The case study classroom typically places a premium on the ability to answer challenges and arguments against expressed positions.

Developing or strengthening effective group participation is another valuable skill enhanced by case method experience. Because case study group discussion proceeds inductively, it is not uncommon for those who see the direction a case is moving or who sense group needs to emerge as valuable group process participants. This skill likewise has value far beyond what it might bring to one meeting or a few classroom case study sessions.

Another important skill that can be developed effectively through case study work is the ability to recognize organizational complexities. Because an individual case can provide only so many details, it is important for students to raise questions—lots of questions—for example, "But what about...?" or "What if...?" or "Are we forgetting that...?"

Finally, those who promote case method learning want students to learn how better to interact and even to disagree with those who see things and draw conclusions different from their individual perspectives. Course instructors will, of course, vary in their expectations, but most will expect—even encourage and nurture—differences of opinion. Reasoned argumentation is also much valued.

Remember, the case study approach is not solely a means of providing information and knowledge; rather, it is interactive, demanding that participants identify, relate, compare, propose answers, and integrate many facets and many ideas from a variety of sources. In addition, the case method helps students develop mature judgments. You will be expected to think actively, to discover that others will interpret and judge differently, to learn the joys of sharing information and insight, to cooperate and pool intellectual efforts with your peers, and to discern that instructors do not own all the answers or even the best answers (Gragg, 1940). A basic element of organizational teamwork is learning to solicit and appreciate the value of individual contributions.

Case Analysis Preparation

Examining for Case Facts

Most instructors who use the case study approach will agree readily with Professor Benson P. Shapiro (1984) of the Harvard Business School, who highlighted students' roles in the case method when he cited the necessity for each student to be committed to the "4 *Ps*" of involvement in case discussions:

1. Preparation. If the student does not read and analyze the case, and then formulate an action plan, the case discussion will mean little to that person.
2. Presence. If the student is not present, she or he cannot learn and, more important, cannot add unique thoughts and insight to the group discussion.
3. Promptness. Students who enter the classroom late disrupt the discussion and deprecate the decorum of the process.
4. Participation. Each student's learning is best facilitated by regular participation. More important, the case student is responsible for sharing her or his understanding and judgment with the class to advance the group's collective skills and knowledge.

Thorough familiarity with the case itself is an essential requisite for preparation. At least two readings of the case are recommended. Ronstadt (1977) encourages a case reading time schedule. The first time through might be a time to gain impressions and become familiar with the overall material. You will want to become acquainted with the structural and stylistic features of the case author(s) and editor(s). Usually the first sections of a case provide situational and organizational contexts. Paragraph leads or section headings might give clues to the case approach. If exhibits or tabular data are included (organizational charts, biographical sketches, statistical compilations), leaf through these as well. Read to get a sense of "What is going on here?" and "How is this case arranged or organized?"

At a second read-through you are ready for slow, careful study. Don't be overanxious to find the "villain" of the situation (Farmer, Richman, & Ryan, 1966). This is the time to make your notes—in your notebook, on note cards, or in the margins of the case text. Here you place your observations and the questions you need to raise (Ronstadt, 1977, p. 7). At this point most students work through the questions at the end of the case and/or additional instructor-assigned questions. The study questions or guides usually are general rather than comprehensive and are not meant to limit your own study. You will be wise to go well beyond those few questions to develop and answer your own.

This second careful examination of the case is the time to identify the problem. For problem analysis, consider these questions:

1. What are the key issues (Ronstadt, 1977, p. 11)?

2. Are there hidden issues?
3. What appear to be current objectives and practices of the organization in the case (Greyser, 1981)?
4. Can I list problem and subproblem factors or questions?
5. Is more information needed to understand the problem?

As the problem or problems are identified, it is usually appropriate to ask yourself "Why was this case assigned now?" Obviously the instructor has some concept or principle in mind. What is it in this particular case that fits your current study of assigned text or related conceptual materials? Remember, complexities and factors in the case could be used to examine more than one concept. Usually you will be aware of the instructor's focus, however, so do not be led astray.

This stage of analysis is also the time to identify and list that which is factual and that which is not. Label the facts and the inferences. Schnelle (1967) recommends concern about the quality of the case, suggesting we ought to have confidence that the facts are indeed facts, to have assurance of the direction and degree of the outcomes (some form of measurement), and to be confident that the facts have relevance to the problem situation.

A common complaint of students trying to achieve thorough analysis and sound judgment about a case is "We don't have enough facts to solve the problem; we don't know enough about the situation" (Myers & Myers, 1982). Do not panic if you also feel this way when you finish your case readings. Managers and decision makers at all levels do not have all the data, either. They routinely make decisions based on partial or incomplete information. When you determine the data included and the data not included, be ready to make some creative assumptions. Ask questions to clarify and extend the facts. Ask questions to make sure you obtain all the contextual aspects that are available. Then state your assumptions and the knowledge or experience base on which you make an assumption. Bursk and Greyser (1973) urge students "not to disagree with the facts but to read between the facts and doubt the judgments and opinions of the people portrayed in the case" (p. xv).

As you define the problem, you will have to support that definition with relevant facts from the case, pertinent and clearly labeled assumptions, and your interpretation of the events and processes portrayed. Careful study, thoughtful analysis, and well-chosen language will be necessary to convey your understanding.

Examining for Problem and Solutions
Your instructor will probably select for your analysis a range of cases presenting differing levels of difficulty. Leenders and Erskine (1978,

pp. 87–89) have described a case difficulty cube format for examining a case. From an analytical perspective, the tasks may vary as follows:

1. Here is a problem; here is a solution. Do you think the solution fits the problem? Are there alternatives to consider?
2. Here is a problem. Give me a reasonable solution.
3. Here is a situation. What are the problems? What are the solutions?

From the conceptual perspective, the concept or principle may:

1. be readily grasped and understood;
2. be understood only by further clarification through class discussion and repetition; or
3. require extensive clarification, instructor involvement, and perhaps more than single exposure.

Finally, from the presentation perspective:

1. the simplest form will have little extraneous material, with data presented neatly and in a straightforward manner;
2. a second degree of difficulty provides an average amount of information, some extraneous data, and normal length; and
3. a third degree contains large amounts of extraneous data and will be relatively unorganized, requiring sorting in preparation for analysis (Leenders & Erskine, 1978).

Whatever degree of difficulty the case presents to you, your problem-solving analysis should be done in advance of any classroom meeting for discussing or demonstrating the analysis. Problem solution likely will be a major activity conducted in the larger group, but individual preparation will be the key to your confidence and readiness to participate.

A basic problem-solving model in use for many years is still recommended by case instructors. Students of communication or business management, as well as others who have taken coursework in small-group discussion or decision making, will recognize the basic scientific method popularized by Dewey. The steps are as follows: (1) statement of the problem, (2) statement of pertinent facts, (3) statement of alternative courses of action, (4) advantages and disadvantages of alternative courses of action, (5) evaluation of advantages and disadvantages, and (6) selection of the "best" alternative (Murray & Von der Embse, 1973; Myers & Myers, p. 326; Schnelle, 1967, p. 38). Some analysts suggest a seventh step: implementing the decision. Another step—beyond implementation—compares "expected with actual results of the decision" (Schnelle, 1967,

p. 39). The latter is an excellent extension when the actual decisions and results of cases are known and can, in fact, be compared.

When formulating the *statement of the problem,* keep the following in mind (Bursk & Greyser, p. xiv; Schnelle, 1967, p. 39):

1. Choose the goals of your analysis carefully.
2. Define your problem parameters or boundaries carefully.
3. Be prepared to work on one problem at a time.
4. Examine the situation from the viewpoints of those involved in the case.
5. Solve the most urgent problem first, using "problem listing," a variation of brainstorming that ranks the problems as very urgent (VU), urgent (U), and not urgent (NU).

When defining the *statement of pertinent facts* of a case, it is often helpful to highlight in the text the most salient factual elements. Be sure to clearly distinguish the facts from the interpretations or assumptions made by characters in the case.

After you have clearly stated the problem and determined the factual elements, prepare a *statement of alternative courses of action* for dealing with the case problems. List all viable alternatives compiled in an objective, brainstorming manner. Then prune the list ideally to three to seven alternatives to pursue at greater length. Consider at least one alternative for each extreme position, plus one of a central or moderate type.

Next, look at the *advantages and disadvantages of alternatives proposed.* Again, brainstorming for each proposal will produce lists to be limited further. Record the alternatives on separate sheets of paper, sections of a chalkboard, or computerized lists Visualize and itemize the consequences of each alternative. You might choose to further subdivide advantages into "known" and "suspected" categories. (This process is an excellent application for computer-assisted sorting, arranging, or general preparation.)

With prepared lists of alternatives and lists of advantages and disadvantages, you are ready to begin the *evaluation of advantages and disadvantages.* Clarify items and look for duplications in your lists. Is each advantage really an advantage? What is the sensitivity to change of each alternative? Is any advantage for a given alternative also an advantage for another choice and, therefore, not unique to just one option? Or, is an advantage of one approach also a disadvantage of another alternative? Eliminate any frivolous or insignificant items that become apparent when all are viewed together. You might also find it helpful to determine the relative importance of advantages or disadvantages by assigning a rank order or point value to each. Remember when looking at potential alternatives that none of them has happened yet, that you are dealing with probabilities. Thus, it is possible to examine each proposal by weighing the "iffiness," the certainty value, the likelihood of occurrence. This factor might also be assigned a weighted value if you decide to quantify the final decision step.

After a thorough analysis and realistic, honest, and careful consideration of the advantages and disadvantages of each alternative, the final decision, *selection of the best alternative,* often emerges fairly cleanly. Schnelle (1967, p. 40) sees no judgment necessary if values are assigned to advantages, disadvantages, probabilities, and so on, and then are computed mathematically. If you decide on the more quantifiable route, a simple summation will point the direction. The key, of course, is to be confident that you have given all factors due and proper weight and consideration in each of the earlier steps.

For many cases it is worthwhile to extend analysis to the step of *implementing the decision.* Frequently, in fact, your case instructor will insist that you include implementation steps in recommendations or solutions. This process extends your thinking from strictly paper solutions to the realities of action. "Right" answers or "good" solutions can be sabotaged if not carefully planned all the way through the implementation stage. Your final planning allows you to ask once more, "How can I secure action that will ensure the occurrence of these advantages?"

Demonstrating Case Analysis

After this serious personal attention to the material in a case, including posing answers to the problem, how will you be expected to demonstrate your intellectual insight and skill in analysis? Instructors commonly use one of two methods to evaluate student mastery: (1) a written analysis, either narrow or broad in focus, or (2) a classroom discussion session or extended problem solution analysis through group participation.

The written analysis is typically used on more complex cases. This assignment might even be a fairly short report that highlights your analyzing, organizing, and integrating skills. The suggestions for organizing and preparing your ideas for in-class discussion can also apply to written case analysis.

The in-class instructional approach entails two formats. The first is a question/answer period with the instructor or facilitator. In this situation you will be expected to respond orally, describing the kind of analysis you have made and the steps you recommend for a decision. Although other students are present, the instructor is weighing your individual contributions. In the second in-class strategy, the instructor observes and evaluates your contributions as you engage in problem solution analysis through small-group discussion. This interaction might take several forms, and both individual and group contributions will be scrutinized.

Preparing Your Analysis

Regardless of the in-class reporting or evaluating approach your instructor uses, numerous suggestions have been made to guide you in preparing your analysis. Ronstadt (1977) offers the following practical hints:

1. Envision how the teacher will diagram or describe what you say.
2. From a complex issue, show how you made a decision or a breakdown into lists or steps.
3. Relate analysis to a common experience the class has shared.
4. Crystalize your analysis to a few simple points.
5. Don't try to memorize. Work from notes, as you might well have questions or cross-examination to interrupt you. (pp. 14–15)

Greyser (1981) suggests additional guidelines for handling cases in oral discussion:

1. Don't rehash case facts—interpret them.
2. Let your listener or reader know your purpose, your direction, your rationale, your point of view [your assumptions].
3. If a decision is called for, make it. State the alternatives and pose new ones.
4. If you recommend additional research, discuss what and why. Show how such information would help.
5. Acknowledge implications—risks, feasibility, probability.
6. Think [organize] before you write or speak. (p. xv)

Preparing to Discuss

At some point in the analysis process, you are almost certain to encounter the interaction of case discussion—with the instructor alone or with others in a class or group. Your preparation for and attitude toward class discussion will largely determine the impression you make on the instructor and, more important, will determine what you really carry away with you in terms of communication skills and analysis and decision-making skills. It is your responsibility to share your analysis. It is your responsibility to subject your ideas to open discussion and even debate. In a challenging case, competing or conflicting points of view will arise. Your thoughtful, thorough, and carefully prepared analysis may well be attacked by those who hold another position or view—likewise thoughtful, thorough, and carefully prepared. Fenn, Grunewald, and Katz (1966) describe the case discussion situation as one in which "the student's task shifts to whether or not he [or she] can support his [or her] views against the counterattacks and disagreements of others in the group...[and] accept cooperatively the merits of his [or her] antagonists' reasoning" (p. 10).

Ronstadt (1977) makes several valuable recommendations about preparing for the discussion period:

1. Understand the process of discussion in your class or group.
2. Determine the discussion role(s) you will play.
3. Be aggressive. You need a strong spirit of participation and willingness to mount an offensive in discussing.
4. Plan to listen carefully and to respond to classmates and instructor.
5. Assess your skills, your capabilities in the subject [heading into the discussion].
6. Assess the skills and capabilities of your classmates—compared to yours.
7. Assess the case instructor's approach and style in case teaching: Who talks? Who answers questions? How does the instructor handle participation? How open is the instructor to disagreements? Does the instructor do all the "wrapping up" of each case and issue?
8. After your assessment, decide where and how best to focus your energy and contributions. (pp. 15–20)

Students who have not explored group interaction contributions and patterns are advised to consult sources that define in greater detail the "task" and "maintenance" or "social-emotional" functions needed during problem-solving sessions. Case study students also need to examine their assumptions about "leader" or "questioner" roles.

General Suggestions for Case Participation

Among the many additional practical hints that could be passed on to case study students, only a handful are included here. These few should suggest other behaviors or other research to the resourceful participant.

First, as a case student, accept your own limitations. You will not be totally objective. Recognize early that you have your own prejudices, limited or narrow experiences, and preconceived ideas that will color your judgments about people and organizations. It is easy simply to assume that your analysis is the correct or best way—to be convinced that all your assumptions are correct (Pigors, 1981). Be careful that you do not fall into the trap of being overconfident as you try to avoid appearing unsure, yet do not shrink from ever disagreeing or raising a dissenting opinion.

Second, instructors might choose from dozens of classroom participation strategies or tactics that assume even greater weight when student evaluations rest so heavily on in-class performance and contributions. It does make a difference, for instance, where you sit so as to have greatest conspicuousness and opportunity for involvement. It does make a difference if you demonstrate your preparation and willingness to handle the instructor's leadoff question. How you handle questions or challenges, how you structure or organize your answers, whether you ask relevant questions that avoid digressions, how you perceive and handle digressions—all these help form the instructor's subjective and objective impressions of you. In addition, analyze your small-group members and determine where you fit in; then make limited but judicious references to your personal experiences.

It will also be useful to chronicle your case experiences over a given course or seminar. Record your observations. Keep a journal with notes for yourself. Summarize issues and procedural notes at the close of every case. Ronstadt (1977, p. 21) suggests preparing a Facts, Ideas, and Generalizations (FIG) list or file immediately at the end of a particular case. These summaries can be checked with the instructor for accuracy and usefulness. The summary might also be helpful in your analysis of the next case or issue.

Finally, there is no standard code of ethics for case method behaviors or patterns; nevertheless, moral issues do affect all who examine case studies. Do not provide information on a specific case to people who have not yet had the case in their classes. Others will not learn if you do the analysis. You will not learn if you insist on borrowing. The inventory or value of good cases will be depleted rapidly when you pass on accumulated knowledge or insights. Generally, the instructor will indicate how much group study is permitted prior to the class session.

Do not seek or provide information about a case situation other than what is given in the case, unless *explicitly* permitted by your instructor. Even if you have inside contacts in the organization identified in the case—or what you believe to be the organization—do not rely on them for additional data. They might not have the same information or "right" answers themselves.

Do not "blow the cover" of a disguised case. You can cause embarrassment to companies or agencies, to your instructor, to case writers and editors, and to yourself by writing or calling an organization for more data or background not cleared for use in a case. When an organization provides a clearance to use a case for instructional or training purposes, you can rely on the fact that the case has been submitted to the organization and approved "as written." Personal contacts in an organization might know little or nothing at all of the sensitive content or confidentiality of a case. You are counseled simply to stay out of the organization, unless your presence is explicitly cleared by the case writer.

Finally, do not be a group parasite, holding back your reading and research because you know others will certainly be prepared. Your classmates will soon see through you, and so will your instructor. Individuals with highly developed oral communication skills or group discussion skills particularly need to guard against the dangers of hitchhiking on the solid research of others (Ronstadt, 1977, p. 44ff). An entire class or seminar group will achieve maximum benefits when each participant prepares thoroughly and freely contributes observations, insights, and judgments.

REFERENCES

Bennett, J. B., & Chakravarthy, B. S. (1978, March/April). What awakens student interest in a case. *HBS Bulletin*, pp. 13–14.

Bursk, E. C., & Greyser, S. A. (1975). *Cases in marketing management.* Upper Saddle River, NJ: Prentice Hall.

Champion, J. M., & Bridges, F. J. (1969). *Critical incidents in management* (rev. ed.). Homewood, IL: Irwin.

Farmer, R. N., Richman, B. M., & Ryan, W. G. (1966). *Incidents in applying management theory.* Belmont, CA: Wadsworth.

Fenn, D. H., Jr., Grunewald, D., & Katz, R. N. (1966). *Business decision making and government policy.* Upper Saddle River, NJ: Prentice Hall.

Gragg, C. I. (1940, October). Because wisdom can't be told. *Harvard Alumni Bulletin*, p. 19.

Greyser, S. A. (1981). *Cases in advertising and communications management* (2nd ed.). Upper Saddle River, NJ: Prentice Hall.

Leenders, M. R., & Erskine, J. A. (1973). *Case research: The case writing process.* London, Ontario: School of Business Administration, University of Western Ontario.

Leenders, M. R., & Erskine, J. A. (1978). *Case research: The case writing process* (2nd ed.). London, Ontario: Research and Publications Division, School of Business Administration, University of Western Ontario.

Murray, J. H., & Von der Embse, T. J. (1973). *Organizational behavior: Critical incidents and analysis.* Columbus, OH: Merrill/Prentice Hall.

Myers, M. T., & Myers, G. E. (1982). *Managing by communication: An organizational approach.* New York: McGraw-Hill.

Pigors, P. (1987). Case method. In R. L. Craig, (Ed.), *Training and development handbook: A guide to human resource development* (3rd ed., pp. 414–429). New York: McGraw-Hill.

Ronstadt, R. (1977). *The art of case analysis: A student guide.* Needham, MA: Lord.

Schnelle, K. E. (1967). *Case and business problem solving.* New York: McGraw-Hill.

Shapiro, B. P. (1984). Hints for case teaching. *HBS Case Services*, Boston: Harvard Business School.

Weilbacher, W. M. (1970). *Marketing management cases.* New York: Macmillan.

Understanding the Organization: Structure, Culture, and Climate

CASE 1
Part A. Inside Microsoft
Part B. Microsoft Revisited

CASE 2
Satellite Systems

CASE 3
Scribe & Send

CASE 4
Part A. Mountain City Schools
Part B. Several Years Later

CASE 1

PART A. INSIDE MICROSOFT*

Paul Andrews

During last fall's United Way campaign at Microsoft, two vice-presidents made a wager on whose division would generate the most contributions. The loser, it was agreed, would have to swim the length of "Lake Bill," a small artificial lake at the Redmond corporate campus named after Bill Gates, cofounder and chairman of the world's No. 1 computer software company.

When the campaign wrapped up, however, there was disagreement about who had won. One division had pulled in more money, but the other had a higher percentage of giving. Statistically, both were claiming victory.

To settle the dispute, it was decided that both had "lost" and would be forced to swim the lake. At noontime on the eventful day, employees crowded around the oversized pond to witness the proceedings. Pranksters, concerned that the lake might be too comfortable despite the 38-degree late-fall chill, threw in chunks of ice to lower its temperature.

First up was the colorful Steve Ballmer, vice-president for systems software, a great quipster who once called Intel's 80286 computer chip "brain-damaged." With dramatic flair, Ballmer slowly stripped down to red bikini shorts, dived in, and splashed his way to the other side.

Following him was Mike Maples, vice president for applications, who had come to Microsoft after 23 years with IBM and conducted a sweeping reorganization credited for improving efficiency and teamwork within the company. Maples removed his suit jacket, watch, and shoes; emptied his pockets; and, attired in a glistening wetsuit, jumped in amid the hoots, howls, and cheers of onlookers.

*The *Seattle Times* "Pacific Magazine"; reprinted by permission of the writer and the *Seattle Times*, original date April 23, 1989.

The incident, which immediately assumed a select place in the pantheon of Microsoft legendry, illustrates one side of the company's carefully fostered corporate culture. People who work there, from division managers to marketers to programmers to free-lancers hired on a per-project basis, describe Microsoft as an exhilarating work environment fed by adrenaline, constant brainstorming, and creative drive. Workers wear whatever they want to the office, set their own hours and, because of the corporate campus' innovative X-shaped buildings configuration, have windowed offices of their own. In warm weather people dine outdoors and are entertained by the multiple talents of fellow workers—jugglers, unicyclists jousting with sticks and garbage-can lids, and live music.

If hunger should threaten to interrupt an important project, each wing is supplied with a fast-food "7-Eleven" equipped with a variety of snacks and beverages, the latter provided free. For fitness buffs, membership in a sports/health club just five minutes away is a bennie. And no one wants for the latest techie toys: Nearly every office has at least two computers—an IBM or work-alike "clone," and an Apple Macintosh—and many have more. It's not uncommon to see half a dozen or more video monitors sitting on shelves and desktops in a single office.

All of this is in addition to considerable rewards—professional and material—associated with employment at Microsoft. Many of those who guided the company through its formative years during the early 1980s became instant millionaires when its stock went public in 1986. Even those who joined Microsoft as recently as two or three years ago now head entire divisions. Evidence of growth is everywhere, from bulldozers working on a new computer complex to workers asking for directions in one of eight sleek new buildings at the headquarters complex. The company, with $600 million in sales and $125 million in profits, nearly doubled in size last year to 2,000 workers at the corporate campus and 3,800 worldwide. Although Gates has cautioned that margins will narrow because of greater focusing on research and development, which don't show immediate results on ledger sheets, few analysts see the company reaching a plateau for some time.

Ask anyone who works there, and they'll tell you roughly the same thing. "Microsoft is a great place to work," they will say, "if you don't mind working a lot."

It is the second part of the equation that casts the only shadow on Microsoft's corporate landscape. There is a difference between having fun and venting nervous energy, between riding an adrenaline high and running on empty, and insiders say the demanding pace and push of the high-tech fast lane eventually extract a heavy toll on workers' well-being. The company's awesome growth—it had just 200 employees as recently as 1983—has produced an inevitable share of winners and losers, and competitiveness remains high as rising stars jockey for control of corporate fiefdoms. Stock options during the company's early growth produced numerous wealthy sub-30-year-olds, and for a while buttons showed up on lapels bearing the inscription FYIFV, standing for "F——— You, I'm Fully Vested." Many of those associated with Microsoft's early success, in fact, have left the company—partly to explore other opportunities, partly because they are financially secure, but also because, they say, Microsoft simply expects too much in human terms from its employees. One former executive has even talked about forming a support group for "recovering" ex-Microsoft workers.

"They have a glamorous reputation and have done some innovative things involving partnerships," says Alene Moris, a Seattle career consultant. "But they also stretch people to unbelievable limits. It's always push, push, push, and the stakes are constantly being raised." A former Microsoft higher-up says derisively, "If Microsoft is a great place to work for a corporation, that speaks pretty badly for most corporations." And an editor who interviewed for a position there came away with the impression that although Microsoft "has a lot of nice qualities to it and the company does many things to create a pleasant environment, work definitely comes first. It's a velvet sweatshop."

The delicate balance between work and human potential at Microsoft is an issue that extends well beyond one company and its employees. Computers are playing an ever-expanding role as the work force changes to a service and information-based economy.

The transition is proving to be a not altogether smooth one.

For the Pacific Northwest, long known as the laid-back quality-of-life capital of the U.S., the high-tech juggernaut holds additional cataclysmic implications. The Eastside's [East of Lake Washington; east of Seattle—Bellevue, Redmond] growing technology corridor has brought high-powered, single-minded new college graduates and industry wunderkinds here from California, New York, and elsewhere for whom work is the elixir of life. Where that leaves the so-called Mount Rainier factor and the Northwest's other amenities is uncertain. "There are programmers at Microsoft," says an editor there, "who after two years have never even been to Seattle."

"Working evenings and weekends is just expected of you here," says one Microsoft supervisor. "Everyone else does it, so you have to as well, just to keep up." Asked about hobbies or outside interests, the typical response of a Microsoft employee is to name a certain activity such as painting, mountain climbing, sailing, or whatever, followed by: "But I don't have much time for it anymore." Sixty-hour work weeks without overtime are common. "They tell you to take comp time, but hardly anyone does," says one worker. "There's just too much to do."

"There's something in the high-tech industry that forces you to work at a pace where you don't have another life," observes Posy Gering, manager of communications at nearby Microrim, a storybook success itself that produces the second-best-selling database software in the world. "I've known ex-Microsoft people here that were driven away by it, and the same people are driven away from here as well."

The impact of this singular approach to life on the Northwest character is hard to quantify in absolute terms, but its presence is being felt in key socioeconomic sectors. The fast lane is taking over: Cars are crowding the highways, housing prices are skyrocketing, production is booming. High-powered professionals are moving here from New York, Chicago, and Los Angeles, bringing with them the infrastructural stresses of an expanding population but also the problem-solving skills, high expectations, and leadership potential needed to address growth problems. "When these people discover there's more to life than debugging code," as one pundit puts it, "you're going to see great things from them."

But Microsoft's work ethic also is very much a product of its cofounder and CEO, Gates, a hands-on, proactive executive referred to as "Chairman Bill" in alternately respectful and irreverent terms. The youngest self-made billionaire in history, Gates, 33, keeps a tight rein on productivity by setting a manically driven example himself and intermittently cheerleading, cajoling, and upbraiding his inner circle of managers to maximize performance. "Bill almost always is there on weekends," says a Gates associate, "and he keeps track of who's there and who isn't. If any of the 40 or 50 key people are missing, he'll call them up and ask, "What's the matter? Why haven't I seen you around?" Much of the corporate campus is lit up and bustling around the clock. Microsoft President Jon Shirley says that Gates "will work till 9 or 10 at night, then go out for some dinner, and will be back on his computer at home answering electronic mail past midnight."

It was Gates' idea to leave parking slots unassigned at Microsoft—a subtle but ingenious device to reward early comers. There are no wall clocks at Microsoft—a phenomenon the company denies has any significance, but one which discourages a punch-clock mentality. "It's like time is irrelevant," observes a recent visitor from Silicon Valley. "What better way to get people to concentrate on their work?"

If "techaholism" sounds like the demonic work of invading space aliens in the bucolic Northwest, they are more E.T. than Darth Vader. Partly because companies see themselves as pioneers on the technological landscape, partly because the word "unions" makes the blood drain from their face, they offer an entire supermarket of carrots to workers who in their own right are high-achievement, self-driven personalities. For anyone interested in being on the cutting edge of the industry, Microsoft is high-tech heaven.

It starts with the woodsy corporate headquarters on the outskirts of Redmond—a relaxed, genial setting evocative of the quiet intellectual industry of a college campus. Informality is the rule: Suits or ties are rare, and everyone, even Gates and Shirley, is referred to by his or her first name. Workers stroll through corridors chatting softly but intently, occasionally in a foreign language (a result of the company's overseas intern program). Groups of two or three will gather in a co-worker's office or in a hallway to engage in a "collective brain dump," high-tech jargon for brainstorming. Offices are decorated with posters, dart boards, inflatable toys, streamers, and quirky personal impedimenta, from fish tanks to motorized mice (a play on the Microsoft mouse, a pointing device for PCs). Until the company grew too big, each terminal was named after a character in "Our Gang" or "Sesame Street."

Another key component of Microsoft's informality is its seductive E-mail (electronic messaging) system, which Shirley says epitomizes the corporate culture at Microsoft. Workers can message each other—even Gates and Shirley—day and night, to and from home or office computers, in an instant communications network that, Shirley notes, "flattens the corporate hierarchy considerably." The sophisticated system displays a queue showing the time and date and sender's "log-on," or nickname, for each message and a brief description of its contents. If there's a drawback, it comes under the heading of too much of a good thing: Nathan Myhrvold, director of advanced development, typically receives 200 messages a day, and is still plowing through a backup queue of some 1,600 messages left over from a three-week hiatus when his wife had twins in January.

"For me the essence of Microsoft is the hallway, where people get together to talk about anything," says Pete Higgins, general manager of the analysis business unit who, dressed in an open-collar shirt and slacks, looks like a summer camp director. "Business gets done, but it's all in a very casual atmosphere. Sometimes I'll go out to lunch and people will say, 'Aren't you working today?' I tell them this is what I wear to the office."

"There's lots of computer companies you can go to work for, but there's no company like Microsoft anywhere in this industry," adds John Neilson, product manager for applications marketing. "You get to work with some of the smartest people around, and everywhere there are great ideas bubbling to the surface. That's what Microsoft is—a company of ideas." As an example he points to Microsoft's innovative in-house press, which has produced a distinctive line of appealingly designed manuals and how-to books as well as, through its Tempus imprint, revived leading out-of-print works on science and technology: "You won't find anything like Microsoft press anywhere else in the industry."

However much pride Microsoft takes in its workplace innovations and gung-ho atmosphere, the company is considerably less forthcoming about the pressures of breakneck deadlines and constant growth. Workers quick to extol the multiple charms of their employer prefaced all negative comments with a request for anonymity, and even ex-Microsoft employees expressed concern about repercussions, since many still have affiliations with Microsoft or the high-tech industry. Halfway through the research for this article, sources began calling back frantic, demanding to know which parts of their statements would be used—the result of a memo from Shirley requesting that any contacts with outside media be sanctioned first by corporate communications. In some cases sources were asked to check with the reporter about what would be printed, and report back to the company their findings.

While this strategy had its Orwellian aspects, it is not surprising for a company so prominent in the high-tech fishbowl as Microsoft. Since the Wild West days of backroom bargaining and intellectual thievery during Silicon Valley's teeth-cutting, where widespread chip thefts led to strip searches and program code took on the aura of crown jewels, the high-tech industry has nurtured a fetish for secrecy and information management. In Microsoft's case, Gates is known as a thin-skinned albeit voracious reader of mass media (as well as biographies and history). "If he sees something he doesn't like in print, he'll call people on the carpet," says one source. Gates has granted selective interviews but was traveling over a two-month period and said to be doing "very little media work" during the preparation of this story. Repeated requests for an interview were denied.

Whether the subject is corporate culture, media sensitivity or market position, much of the Microsoft persona can be attributed to simple growing pains. Just 14 years old, if the company were a basketball player, it would be able to look down at the rim. Whatever else can be said about Gates, as a pure businessman he has the Midas touch, and that doesn't mean mufflers. At each juncture of the burgeoning PC industry, Microsoft has made savvy, far-reaching decisions guaranteed to expand profitability and market position. In a make-or-break industry with more losers than an $8 million Lotto, Microsoft's record has been impeccable.

Nevertheless, as industries go, both Microsoft and personal computing are in their infancy. Change happens so apocalyptically that stars incinerate like meteors and millions can be lost on a seemingly minor decision. The flip side of suddenly having it all is knowing you can lose it just as fast.

Perhaps that factor, more than any singular work ethic or corporate policy, explains the state of constant liftoff at companies like Microsoft. "They know that they're not producing something that will be needed in 10 years—in fact, by the time they finish producing something it may be obsolete," says a leading financial adviser to high-tech investors, including several at Microsoft. Partly because of that, and the realization they may not be able to keep up their current pace forever, they tend to be conservative investors "more comfortable in traditional programs of bonds, CDs and tax-free issues," the adviser says.

This sense of stewardship may also explain, to a certain degree, Microsoft's limited community involvement—the company has yet to assume prominence in charity and arts circles. One arts activist blames this on Microsoft's "essentially nerdy personalities—they don't have a lot of social skills or a very balanced view of life," says Bonnie Tabb, corporate affairs assistant who previously was Gates' personal assistant. "The company doesn't want to be in the position of the Bank of America, which cut its [corporate giving] budget from $50 million to $5 million in just one year." Arts and charity support will come as the work force matures, she says: "Microsoft draws a lot of people from cultural centers like New York, and they have very high expectations of the symphony, theater, and arts."

If workplace progressivism and corporate philanthropy seem a lot to ask of a youthful industry, they are not ideals inconsistent with Microsoft's vision of itself. Over and over, comparisons between it and the Northwest's other leader in American industry—the Boeing Co.—pop up in conversations. Both companies achieved early and prominent success, and both are net exporters. Of all major software companies, Microsoft is in the best position to eventually achieve the kind of hegemony in its field that Boeing enjoys in commercial aircraft.

To do so, however, the company will have to keep attracting the best and brightest of its profession, and hang on to them. As its work force matures—the median age is just 30 partly because Microsoft hires so many recent college graduates—the company will be forced to address career issues with the same innovative, problem-solving approach that led it to the pinnacle of its industry. Already it has experimented with alternatives: Jeff Harbers, a 36-year-old manager of data-access business units who's been with the company since 1981, is in the middle of an open-ended leave of absence; another manager served a sort of "in-house fellowship," meeting with software users and vendors to plumb marketing suggestions, after the arrival of a new baby in his household.

"Programs are getting tremendously more complex, forcing the product development cycle to lengthen," Harbers notes. "We're going to have to set expectations so people don't feel way behind all the time. And if you're planning on being around for 40 years, you have to give people more in life than just their work."

In a larger context, Microsoft's workforce issues are the same as those for many of the achievement-oriented, high-pressure Baby Boom professionals who during the 1980s embraced work as their badge of identity but are now having to reevaluate its impact on their personal lives, friendships, and family and life goals. Companies where employees typically work 10- or 12-hour days are experimenting with four-day work weeks, mental health days, and work-at-home options, simply so workers have time to look after personal affairs.

"There's so much excitement at companies like Microsoft, it's addictive—the workers become hooked," says Alene Moris. "It isn't until they get sick or make a big mistake on the job or are confronted by an angry or neglected spouse or romantic partner that they finally can step back and evaluate. In a way they need to recognize the fact that growing this fast is not wise, but I don't know how you can teach any American that."

It's a ticklish proposition for any fast-moving company: keeping workers motivated, creative, and energized while still offering them the chance for a balanced, self-nurturing existence. As big as its corporate map has grown and promises to keep growing, all roads at Microsoft still lead back to one source. An insider puts it this way: "If Bill Gates would just get married," she says with a sigh, "then I think you'd see a big change."

C A S E 1

PART B. MICROSOFT REVISITED

Gary L. Peterson

A recent stroll across the main Microsoft campus in Redmond, Washington, would most likely show a view that looks remarkably like a well-kept university campus: clusters of buildings, beautiful expanses of grassy areas, a softball field here, a tent going up for a picnic there, and maps and direction markers at each intersection. There might be, at nearly any time of day, a group of young people tossing Frisbees, using that softball field, or a group of jugglers on the mall. The idyllic serenity is broken by the sight of large cranes and construction barriers at different spots around the grounds.

But this is no ordinary campus. In addition to the thirty-eight Headquarters complex buildings are another fourteen buildings owned domestically. Microsoft, at age twenty-three, also lists 113 U.S. Domestic Leased Sites, including large product support centers in North Carolina and Texas. One hundred seventy-six additional leased and nine owned international operations sites can be found in over sixty countries ranging from China to Dubai, Croatia, Russia, Romania, and Uruguay. Indeed, Microsoft business is fueled heavily by international sales—some 56 percent of revenues now coming from overseas (year ending December 1998).

Microsoft's campus is different in other ways as well. Most offices are a similar size, but each seems to be treated as an individually decorated enclave, as if proclaiming proudly, "I may have to move again in a few weeks, but this is my place, and what I put here is my personality." The campus is wired technology personified. E-mail has long been extensively used, as has voice mail. A highly developed Intranet web calls up hundreds of thousands of details about the company, anything from hourly stock prices to building and room diagrams.

Conversations are regularly laden with Microsoft and software tech jargon: "net-net," "drill down," "bandwidth," "off-line," "push back" were but a handful of the phrases readily provided as examples of commonplace Microsoft terminology. Employees are also a frequent source of techie "TLAs."

Microsoft by the close of 1998 employed over 30,200 workers worldwide, two-thirds in the United States. With growth and maturity, structure and organization have changed—often—but have retained important visionary roots. John Shirley and Mike Maples, early key senior officers, have left the company, but they bestowed a legacy of standard setting, organizational structure, and efficiencies that are still widely acknowledged. As large as Microsoft has grown, even the company picnic has now moved off the main campus. An entire sales force meeting in New Orleans recently drew over 6,000 people from worldwide spots. The most recent annual employees meeting was attended by over 9,600 employees in Seattle's Kingdome (ironically doomed for demolition to make way for a new stadium for Microsoft cofounder Paul Allen's football team, the Seahawks). The company Christmas party, however, has also been a victim of growth, having moved from several floors of the Westin Hotel in Seattle, to the Washington State Convention Center straddling Interstate 5 through downtown, and now relegated to individual project or business group parties for employees and families.

Indeed, the maturing of Microsoft has changed even the intensity of the pressure to work so much. "The precious commodity now is time," reported one Microsoft manager recently, an employee who was a rebounder, having left Microsoft with a company colleague to form a new business venture. They had some success, he said, but after selling his share of the new company, he was happy to be back at Microsoft, where exciting things keep occurring and where there are opportunities and challenges to shift focus and do something different. In fact, the variety of work at Microsoft seems to be one of the major appeals. Employees often change assignments and projects. There are twenty-somethings at Microsoft who have already done the globe-trotting cycle of traveling across the world delivering workshops and seminars to groups of 40 to 400. Now they are back at HQ, doing more sedate things such as leading small groups of chief financial and operating officers of major corporations in the Microsoft Executive Briefings boardroom.

There still are no wall clocks at Microsoft, still no reserved parking spots, although valued carpool signs and disabled parking areas are commonplace. There is still a very competitive drive among work groups internally—as much as there is a corporate drive to be the best, to be at the top. The expectation of working late and putting in extremely long hours is reportedly diminished but has not disappeared. Development deadlines, "shipping dates," and decreased time in developing the newest version of virtually every product all still drive a pace that pushes the work cycle (but not overtime—except for contract employees, of whom there are many).

That Microsoft harnesses the time and energy of these bright, creative, and productive young employees is a testimony to its recruitment and hiring practices. It now does more recruiting among MBA graduates and uses headhunters to identify people to join part of the $2 billion R and D program. Some critics warned that Microsoft might be hard-pressed to hire 2,500 new workers needed in the 1998–99 period, because it had reached a size and an age that makes it too corporate, and because many who might otherwise apply could be wary of the predatory image of the company (Mitchell, 1998). The company unabashedly acknowledges that it looks for the talented and creative. These new hires join others who are largely self-driven, and thus employees continue to build a culture where few limits have been set, where there is no lack of projects or desire or reward. Perhaps not so remarkably, many employees who have become relatively wealthy through Microsoft stock and stock options at an early age stay on "not because they have to work at Microsoft" but because this is their world, and they still want to contribute to progress and improvement. Newer challenges clearly are to work smarter. Because Microsoft subsidizes connecting lines to home, there is also proportionately more telecommuting to accomplish work at home yet still enjoy family or relationship time. While salaries and benefits are less a driver for those who have been at Microsoft for some time, "what you have to remember," one employee cautioned, "is that there are still a lot of hungry young people here, probably more young workers in total numbers than there has ever been. The mind-set of the younger workers still drives accomplishment" (just under 30 percent of U.S. employees in 1998 were ages twenty to twenty-nine). Microsoft employees appear to talk much less of a "velvet sweatshop" and more of what they term a "golden handcuff."

In keeping with the 1990s culture and the slightly aging workforce at the company (the 1998 average age in the United States was 34.4), more employees are married with children. There are many dual-Microsoft couples, and the company has been liberal in applying benefits to domestic partners. More employees now live in Seattle and do the reverse commute eastward across Lake Washington every morning. More employees now belong to a diversity of internal groups: BAM (Blacks at Microsoft), GLEAM (Gays and Lesbians at Microsoft), and other ethnic or special identity affiliations.

Perhaps the most striking change in Microsoft as a twenty-three-year-old club with several millionaires has been their impact on their community—the economics, the lifestyle, the environment, philanthropy. Their steady growth has filled corporate HQ parking lots, while helping make parking lots out of adjoining streets and highways.

Microsoft recognizes it has helped power an economic boomlet, but it also knows it is part of the problem. It has created an extensive shuttle system between the main campus and its close satellites. It rewards carpooling, subsidizes bus passes, guarantees taxi rides home if kept late on a project, and its employees sit on community planning and transportation boards. The Microsoft campus has been beautifully kept, and though no longer so "woodsy," it is groomed and greened.

As predicted, arts and charity support have indeed come with the maturing of the company and the workforce. Microsoft's first "Giving Program" netted $17,000. In the last full reported year (1997), giving increased 26 percent over the previous year, reaching a total of $14 million given to charitable and nonprofit groups. More than two-thirds of Microsoft employees participated in the company's matching gifts program, which matches employee contributions up to $12,000 per year. Over 3,500 nonprofit groups received over $12.5 million in cash and $10 million in software donations (*Micro News*, 1998). Indeed, Microsoft in 1999 received United Way's annual "Spirit of America" award, signifying the single American business exceeding all others in corporate community involvement.

The company will continue to donate software to a national philanthropic program, Libraries Online, which takes PC technology and Internet access to public libraries. Bill and Melinda Gates have personally taken over the pledge of $200 million to expand that program to libraries serving low-income communities in the United States and Canada. Gates has also recently made news by making major donations to the nearby University of Washington, as well as to Harvard University and a major research center for Oxford University in England.

Even more significantly, employees and former employees have been founding their own charitable groups and foundations to support community efforts. A recent Puget Sound area story explored but a few of those: Ida Cole, who gave millions to help save the Paramount Theater in downtown Seattle; Scott Oki's Oki Foundation, which gives away nearly $500,000 a year, mostly to children's causes; Trish Millines, a thirty-nine-year-old retiree who created a foundation to help train minority children in computers (Roberts, 1997).

The giving effort has been ambitious and remarkable, with yearly goals constantly increasing. And employees can afford it—apparently individually, and certainly on the corporate side. Microsoft's corporate revenues were up 28 percent for FY 98, to $14.48 billion; income after taxes was up even more (39 percent) to $4.49 billion (*Microsoft Fast Facts*). Microsoft touts a company group tasked with the investment and management of what had reached, by the end of 1998, a total of $19.2 billion. By the end of September 1998 Microsoft's market capitalization had passed General Electric into the first spot, with $240 billion, to GE's $235 billion.

A little perspective: in 1990 Microsoft first reached $1 billion in sales, by 1994 $4.65 billion; IBM's 1998 market capitalization was at one point $120 billion and General Motors a mere $33 billion. Almost since the company went public in 1986 and started to turn handsome profits, executives have warned that the company could not keep up the trend. Analysts largely have not believed them—and with reason. With its relentless aggressiveness in pursuing more and more ways to engage the globe—in financial transactions, in news, in entertainment, in databases, in communications, in Internet—Microsoft has steadily bought or partnered into technology that has positioned it to be a player in most ventures on its playing field.

The corporation has, of course, been widely criticized for its hardball approach to takeovers and partnerships and pressing deals with computer or component manufacturers. Recent history of the "Internet wars" has Microsoft in one very familiar role: that of picking up market share in Internet business and being vilified by comments from competitors. A second role is less familiar: not just being the target of jilted partners or potential partners but feeling the pressure of the federal government in the form of antitrust lawsuits. This situation has become a longer shadow, sapping a tremendous amount of time and energy of Microsoft's corporate legal department. What many now fear is that Microsoft could somewhere in the future be "the universal gatekeeper of thought" (Andrews and Flores, 1997). Competitors in Silicon Valley have spoken and acted on the basis of "Anyone but Microsoft" as they entered into businesses and developments (Andrews, 1998).

These legal troubles have kept Microsoft employees from top to bottom rather touchy about criticism and negative stories. Ever more careful about being the "top dog" or, more typically, "the target," employees who have been provided with a great deal of ownership and responsibility, in addition to their material benefits, have been naturally reluctant to sound ungrateful. Most, like their top officers, are unrepentant about Microsoft's mostly victorious, stunning run of successes. "Now," many employees say, "we feel the pressure of no longer being regarded as the darling of the industry, the 'new guy.' Now, we're the bad guy."

Steve Ballmer, now president, increasingly has been the preacher of greater customer attention and greater internal communication. Moreover, he has increasingly been the point man in Microsoft directions and has battled competitors and an unfriendly Federal Department of Justice. Chairman Bill Gates too, has warned the company of complacency and lack of motivation. While he may have become less at the forefront in company day-to-day affairs, and while he may now be a family man with a young daughter, he has not slowed down and still represents the vision of the company. He has been seen to jet about more, to host corporate, media, and government leaders at his new $53 million mansion on Lake Washington. He has continued to promise he will give away most of his billions, but readers are urged to read or view the Gates address at the 1998 Microsoft annual meeting. He closed that presentation saying the company was "still very much in the beginning" of what it will ultimately accomplish. "Our work," he said, "has not changed the way people do things nearly as much in the last twenty-five years as it will in the next ten" (*Micro News*, 1998).

QUESTIONS FOR DISCUSSION

1. What distinctive differences can be seen in Microsoft's formative stages and in how its culture appears to be evolving? How do you account for those changes?
2. Both in early organizational life and in a maturing stage, what organizational norms, beliefs, values, or customs at Microsoft seem to be communicated informally? What elements are communicated formally?
3. How do organizational stories, symbols, and assumptions reveal Microsoft's philosophies, purposes, and goals?
4. Based on how things have altered over a brief period, what would you try to do as you went into Microsoft Corporation now to identify the status symbols for its employees? The specialized vocabulary or jargon necessary to understand what is going on? The way decisions are made? The expectations for achievement and success?
5. As Microsoft has continued to grow in size and the extent of operations, what cultural elements do you believe it has tried to cultivate and retain? To change? Why?

REFERENCES

Andrews, P. (1998, January 25). Steve Ballmer: Microsoft's heir apparent. *Seattle Times*, p. A1.

Andrews, P., & Flores, M. M. (1997, March 9). Internet wars: Can Microsoft rule the web? *Seattle Times*, p. A1.

Micro News. (1998, September 25). pp. 1,5.

Microsoft Fast Facts. (1998). [Online]. Available: http://www.microsoft.com/presspass/fastfacts.htm#year

Mitchell, R. (1998, October 19). Microsoft's mid-life crisis. *US News Online* [Online]. Available: http://www.usnews.com/usnews/issue981019/19micr.htm

Roberts, C. R. (1997, July 6). Microsoft's millionaires pile up philanthropy. *News Tribune*, pp. B1, B3.

Sullivan, N. (1998). How to get bought by Microsoft (and other things they don't teach you in Business School). *PC Computing* [Supplement]. (pp. 12–17). New York: ZD.

SELECTED BIBLIOGRAPHY

Barley, S. R. (1983). Semiotics and the study of occupational and organizational cultures. *Administrative Science Quarterly, 28,* 393–413.

Barnett, G. A. (1988). Communication and organizational culture. In G. M. Goldhaber & G. A. Barnett (Eds.), *Handbook of organizational communication* (pp. 101–130). Norwood, NJ: Ablex.

Deal, T. A. (1986). Deeper culture: Muckraking, muddling, and metaphors. *Training and Development Journal, 40,* 32–33.

Eisenberg, E. M., & Riley, P. (1988). Organizational symbols and sense-making. In G. M. Goldhaber & G. A. Barnett (Eds.), *Handbook of organizational communication* (pp. 131–150). Norwood NJ: Ablex.

Schein, E. H. (1986). What you need to know about organizational culture. *Training and Development Journal, 40,* 30–31.

Wallace, J., & Erickson, J. (1991, May 6–10.). Bill Gates: Of mind and money. *Seattle Post-Intelligencer* [five-part newspaper series].

Wallace, J., & Erickson, J. (1992). *Hard drive: Bill Gates and the making of the Microsoft empire.* Somerset, NJ: Wiley.

SATELLITE SYSTEMS

Scott Hammond

It was 9 A.M. and time for the staff meeting, but the VIP wasn't there. Satellite Systems Vice President and General Manager Bill Curtis noticed that this meeting was different from the usual weekly affair. He could see each manager was dressed a little sharper, and the coffee was being served in "real" cups. The participants from the different departments in the satellite uplink company were going through their wallets, showing each other their cards. One suggested that before starting they pledge allegiance to the plaque on the wall. After twenty minutes the VIP from corporate came in. He was Robert Vallet, CEO of the communications holding company. He was dressed like a CEO, or at least a Wall Street banker. Lean in appearance, he also had the reputation for being lean on risk. "A bottom-line man," Curtis had heard Vallet call himself.

Today's meeting did not have the usual agenda of business-related items. Instead, Robert Vallet stood and talked about the greatness of the company, the bright future of the organization, and the pride each manager should feel. The group of twenty managers listened politely and intently. They did not want to disagree or take issue. Vallet did not invite the other fifty technical workers in the company. Bill Curtis had suggested inviting them, but Vallet had said he wanted to meet with the "movers and shakers" and not a bunch of technicians. To Bill, who was an engineer by training, these technical workers were the heart of the company. He knew that the technicians and staff workers were talking about the "big wig" meeting and that whatever information they did not get soon would be fabricated by the grapevine anyway.

Vallet continued to talk, but Curtis was only half-listening. Only the day before over lunch Curtis had reviewed the state of the company with this same group. Most had agreed that morale was at an all-time low.

"It's like the soup of the day around here," said one experienced and senior technical manager. "We get a new program every six months that is supposed to make us better people and create a better company. But it's really just window dressing. They don't want to address the real issues." Another technical manager complained that the organization had not caught up with the technology. She said, "They want a one-size-fits-all program in this company, but the reality is that we are very different from our sister divisions. They are really show biz with a little technology built in. But we are truly a technology company. Our success is based on how we stay on or create the leading edge. If we fall behind, our customers are gone in 90 days."

Bill's mind wandered as he thought of the frustrations of his people. He could think of five or six "effectiveness programs" that had come from corporate over the last six years. Though "required," they had no apparent relevance to the company's circumstances or conditions. In addition to these half-dozen programs, he knew there were others he was forgetting. This new program that Vallet was pushing, however, seemed to have more emphasis than the others—perhaps because Vallet himself was relatively new and did not have a real history with the firm.

Overall, Bill was proud of his division. Despite the problems of a rapid, ever-changing technology, he believed his group had adapted well. Most of the competition had gone under or merged in the last few years, leaving Satellite Systems smaller and more agile than the remaining bunch. Bill liked to think they were closer to the clients' needs than their competitors. In fact, Bill knew most of their major clients on a first-name basis. He was not above going to lunch with one of his account managers who was meeting with a client. Contrary to what some of the managers felt about this practice initially, Bill's presence usually made the account managers feel important, showing that they were on a first-name basis with the vice president. And the clients felt more important, too.

In the conference room Vallet talked about the corporate-wide values program. He said he believed it had been a great success. He said the company had come to represent the values of fairness, honesty, and integrity to the customer and to the employees: "We are a people company and we are proud of it." As part of the program, headquarters issued plaques to every division with the values statement inscribed. The CEO said he was glad to see that there was a plaque in this very room. Bill Curtis scanned the room. On the faces of all, he could see the outward evidences of that sense of pride, but he knew it was not genuine.

Bill knew, for example, that the conference room white board usually covered the plaque—except when there was a corporate visitor. Then there were the cards. As if on cue, CEO Vallet continued by asking each of the employees to hold up the "values card" that each was expected to carry in pocket or purse. Twenty out of twenty managers held up their cards. Bill had to smile wryly, knowing that the grapevine from other divisions was working. They had been warned at Satellite Systems to expect that the CEO would ask to see the cards. Some had dug through their desks to find the unused card. Bill himself had to borrow one from his secretary.

"I believe that if we all keep these corporate values before us, we will treat our people better and have a better company!" Vallet paused for effect, and it was something less than he expected. There was polite applause, however, and then the CEO sat down. Bill rose and asked if there were any questions. That, he felt, was at least a polite gesture. He did not really expect any questions and silently prayed that there would be none. Wouldn't you know, though, that one of the younger, outspoken sales managers piped up. "We've spent a lot on a new uplink system this year, and now we learn that it won't be on-line until the middle of the fourth quarter. Our customers simply aren't buying because they can't see it working yet. Because of that," he stumbled a little, apparently realizing he was now getting to the sticky spot, "because of that, sales revenues are down. What should we do?"

This particular issue had been the major, most hotly debated topic of the last five staff meetings at Satellite Systems. Members of the salesforce were concerned because they were losing needed commissions, but everyone agreed fully that if they could just get the new system on-line, there would be plenty of commissions and plenty of other work to go around. Meanwhile, it was not just rumored: the company, admittedly, was borderline in the red.

Robert Vallet rose to his full CEO height and responded directly to the brave questioner: "If you can't sell this thing, then we will get someone who can!" There were no more questions.

QUESTIONS FOR DISCUSSION

1. What are the cultural values at Satellite Systems relative to communication? To technology? To information flow? To openness? How do these values differ from those of the larger corporation?
2. Should the parent company try to change the culture? Could it change the culture?
3. What role did Bill Curtis and Robert Vallet play in managing the organizational culture?
4. What are the differences between the espoused culture and the practiced culture? Is such disparity harmful?
5. Consider how you would role-play a conversation between Bill Curtis and Robert Vallet the day following the CEO's visit. What should Curtis tell Vallet? How should Vallet respond?

SELECTED BIBLIOGRAPHY

Martin, J. (1985). Can organizational culture be managed? In Peter J. Frost et al. (Eds.), *Organizational culture* (pp. 95–98). Beverly Hills, CA: Sage.

Smircich, L. (1983). Implications for management theory. In L. L. Putnam & M. E. Pacanowsky (Eds.), *Communication and organizations: An interpretive approach* (pp. 221–242). Beverly Hills, CA: Sage.

Smircich, L., & Calas, M. B. (1987). Organizational culture: A critical assessment. In F. M. Jablin et al. (Eds.), *Handbook of organizational communication: An interdisciplinary perspective* (pp. 228–263). Beverly Hills, CA: Sage.

See also "Organizational Culture" chapters or sections in recent editions of organizational communication textbooks.

SCRIBE & SEND

Gretchen Rauschenberg

Scribe & Send is a small chain of service outlets in the lower Midwest of the United States. Each branch offers typing and other office services as well as mailing services of all types. Clients are typically blue-collar families who need help with government forms and have occasional need for desktop publishing, posters, or special mailings. Early in the development of this business, many of the customers were migrant farm workers and other manual laborers who needed help applying for Social Security or filling out other governmental applications. The owner is the grandson of a Mexican *escribano*—a public scribe who performed such services for illiterates and also wrote love letters for his customers.

The original office is on the fringe of East St. Louis, and it remains the central office for the fourteen branch offices located in a five-state region. The offices are located in villages or small strip malls, with spartan furnishings and friendly workers recruited locally. Each office is supervised by someone who has been with Scribe & Send for at least three years and who has expertise in one or more of the services offered. At least one employee in each branch is skilled at desktop publishing. Most branches have at least one employee trained in graphic arts—usually the same employee who does the desktop publishing jobs. The typical employee has a high school education and learns on the job how to do whatever is needed by the customers.

Scribe & Send branches are also pickup points for Federal Express and United Parcel Service, and most have postal substations. Some customers maintain mail pickup boxes there. Customers can use Macintosh or IBM-compatible computers at an hourly rate, but most prefer that Scribe & Send's employees do the computer work. High-speed copy machines and fax machines are available in each branch, but only employees are trained and allowed to use them. Customers use coin-operated copy machines.

Employees are paid a base hourly rate but are also paid a commission if the volume of the work they handle justifies their time. Some jobs. have special reward incentives. For instance, when the graphic artist prepares posters and pamphlets and contracts for a bulk mailing, all using the same design, she or he receives a small bonus.

Repeat business is critical for this relatively small operation. Customers are valued and are regularly encouraged to return and to send their friends. Productivity, likewise, is important. Typing and data-entry jobs must be done with speed and accuracy. Teamwork is encouraged, yet the quality of each job is the responsibility of the individual worker handling that particular account or project.

The owner of Scribe & Send is Juan Carlos Molino, son of the founder. Molino still meets customers, weighs mail, and is able to do any of the jobs in any office. He is friendly yet firm with his supervisors but distant from the employees in other branches. Branch supervisors travel to East St. Louis each Tuesday morning for a meeting with Molino. They return to their offices on Tuesday afternoon, bringing supplies and incentives to those who work in the branches they supervise.

Neither Molino nor any branch supervisor works in a private office. All employees share the open space of the storefront, using desks or work areas as needed for the job at hand. Chairs for customers are scattered through the area. The only counter is at the postal substation; a cash register there serves the entire business.

One Tuesday afternoon, supervisors return from their weekly meeting with instructions to crack down on the hourly work schedule and to send copies of the schedule to the main office a month in advance. Previously, schedules were always handled at the branch, and employees could (and regularly did) trade hours informally. Also, all employees are to be motivated to sell a new service: accepting payments for credit cards and other bills. In addition, Molino wants each branch to develop a special Christmas advertising mailing with coupons and special offers from its bulk mailing customers.

Ann is supervisor of a rural office in the town of Chia, Missouri. When she arrives at the store on Tuesday afternoon, she informally announces to the employees that she has further information to share with them.

Ann: We need to have a meeting for all employees at 6:30 when the branch closes. I've got some tough news for us all, and I want to tell everyone at once.

Joe: Sorry, I can't stay today. I already promised to be somewhere else.

Mary: I already have to stay late to finish this job. Can't the meeting wait until Wednesday?

Agnes: Tell us now and get it over with. There aren't any customers here at the moment.

Ann: It's too complicated for a time when we are open to the public. Would you rather come in at 7:45 tomorrow morning?

All: NO!

At 6:30, after the last customer has left, Joe is standing with his coat on as Ann begins the meeting.

Ann: I really want your input on this matter. How can we handle the work schedule so that it works for us, and so that we can send it to the boss two weeks in advance?

Mary: He just doesn't understand! We need to stay flexible. One of the reasons I work for these crummy wages is that I can adjust the hours around my kids' needs.

Joe: Ann, just work it out and send it in, and then we can keep on doing what we've always done.

Ann: No, Juan Carlos will be computerizing the payroll and needs to have the hours into the system early so that we can be paid on time. Our flexible approach won't work out fairly for everyone in terms of accurate pay records.

Joe: Will he always pay on time now? None of those late checks like last month? I don't believe it! I'm out of here!

Ann: Joe, wait. We have something else we all need to talk about. There is to be a big advertising push in our local papers, paid for out of the central office, for local Christmas specials. We are to sell our customers and potential customers on the idea of offering specials, coupons, and so on, in a bulk mail promotion package.

Agnes: I don't mind designing the coupons, but I hate to sell. That's why I didn't go into business for myself as a desktop publisher. If someone else will sell the ads, I'll be happy to produce the copy.

Joe: Let me know what you decide to do. I'm leaving. [And he did just that, closing the door behind him.]

Jim: Ann, do we have to do this today or tomorrow? Juan Carlos isn't being realistic if he springs something like this on us and expects immediate changes. I really do need to do another half-hour's work, and I want to get home ASAP.

Ann: You'll find my instructions about this sales campaign on your desks when you get to work tomorrow. Please give me a memo by Friday about your first choice of firm working hours. I'll consult with each of you during the day Friday. I also need from each of you a list of potential advertisers for the Christmas special. OK, we'll call it a day, unless anyone wants to stay and help me outline the campaign goals.

Ann didn't even have a chance to mention the bill-paying service. She talked to the employees individually the next day and informed them about the new service soon to be offered. It was two weeks later when the store employees next met together. This time, Ann announced the meeting several days in advance, and everyone stayed late.

Ann: We are the only office that didn't have a permanent work schedule submitted by last week. I must have your input before you go home today, or you will have to work the hours I assign you, with no changes.

Sherri: I missed the last meeting because Tuesday isn't a day I work. What's this all about? Why didn't you just tell him we wouldn't do it? I mean, we've always worked things out without his 'help' before.

Joe: I've been thinking about this. What if we did work it out six weeks ahead and put it on the bulletin board. Then we'd have two weeks to trade hours before the final version had to go in.

Ann: How does that sound to the rest of you?

Agnes: If he knows about it, he's going to require it two months ahead. I wish his father was still in charge. He didn't try to put everything into a big-business mentality. I mean, what does it matter about hours set in advance? We still get paid by the timecards, when we punch in and out.

Ann: I'm not sure why he wants these so far ahead. Do any of the rest of you have thoughts on this? Do you want to try Joe's idea?

All: It probably won't work, but it's worth a try.

Ann: Now, about the Christmas promotion. The three supervisors in rural offices seem to be having more problems with it than those near big cities. We're about middle-range in what we've accomplished. Any suggestions for improving our volume? There is a financial bonus for excelling in results.

Sherri: What works in the cities doesn't work here. We can't run a coupon special on farm products! We have limited possibilities, that's for sure.

Mary: You know, I was wondering if we could advertise in it ourselves? We could do Christmas cards for people, especially the photo card variety. Or we could give them a coupon for half-price on Christmas letters done in the color copies. Or, maybe...no, that wouldn't work.

Jim: What was your other idea?

Mary: Maybe we could offer a personalized shopping service, and hire some part-timers. I mean, look, there's no place around here to earn extra bucks for Christmas. Some farm wives whose kids are in school could take orders and go in to the big mall during the day with shopping lists from people like me who do work and never have time to buy toys for the kids. I get to the mall on weekends, but the kids are always along. I'd pay someone to go stand in line to buy some stuff.

Joe: Sounds like a complicated thing to work out.

Mary: Not very. Make a few phone calls. Sign up people willing to shop if they were paid mileage and so much an hour. Then print a coupon for twice the rate, but at a discount. Then we'd be getting something and so would our special shoppers.

Ann: I dunno. Let me talk to Juan Carlos about it.

QUESTIONS FOR DISCUSSION

1. Do the employees think Ann is representing them and their needs at the weekly supervisors' meeting?
2. What was the result of the unannounced meeting held on Tuesday evening? What differences in productivity were evident at the announced meeting?
3. How would you compare the communication climate in the branch office with the communication climate between the branch and the central office?
4. What suggestions might improve the communication climate between the central office and the branches?
5. How does the branch office climate communicate to customers that this is a comfortable, nonoverpowering place to do their copying, word processing, and other paperwork?

SELECTED BIBLIOGRAPHY

Falcione, R. L., Sussman, L. & Herden, R. P. (1987). Communication climate in organizations. In F. Jablin et al. (Eds.), *Handbook of organizational communication: An interdisciplinary perspective* (pp. 195–227). Beverly Hills, CA: Sage.

Poole, M. S. (1985). Communication and organizational climates: Review, critique, and a new perspective. In R. D. McPhee & P. K. Tompkins (Eds.), *Organizational communication: Traditional themes and new directions* (pp. 79–108). Beverly Hills, CA: Sage.

CASE 4

PART A. MOUNTAIN CITY SCHOOLS

Gary L. Peterson

Mountain City, population in excess of 165,000, is a western urban setting where the schools are in transition—and, according to some, in trouble. School enrollments are declining, buildings aging, staff graying, and morale sagging.

Mountain City Schools (MCS) are clearly an urban district, with fairly extensive culturally diverse populations: Asian American, African American, and American Indian. The district serves approximately 29,500 students in five high schools (plus an alternative school), ten junior high schools, forty elementary schools, and a vocational/technical program for post–high school education. Current school district staffing numbers are 1,825 certificated personnel (teachers, administrators, supervisors, librarians, professionals), and 1,395 classified employees (technical, secretarial, custodial, maintenance, transportation, etc.). There are sixty-two work sites across the city. The school district negotiates with fourteen different bargaining agent groups, the largest being Mountain City Educators Association (MCEA), which represents primarily teaching staff. Central school district administrative offices commonly are referred to as "The Hill."

Community support for MCS historically has been excellent. Voters routinely pass bond and levy issues. Recently, however, such support has slipped, occasioned at least in part by considerable publicity about how Mountain City students are performing below national means on some standardized tests. Levels of financial support received from the state are an ongoing concern. Routinely, K–12 educational funds are a source of political football. Uncertainty about funding levels and about salary policies/increases has resulted in demonstrations and trips to the state capitol by organized labor groups and by district administrators and boards. The near-constant media attention has stirred action in the community, and school staff members increasingly have expressed concern.

THE SITUATION

During the past spring MCS's superintendent, Dr. Kenneth Dokens, determined to address the increasing levels of concern expressed by district employees. Dokens engaged district specialists along with outside consultants to conduct an extensive survey to determine employee attitudes about school district policies and practices. The research was undertaken as a preliminary to long-range planning efforts. The researchers pored over a large amount of data from written surveys (2,072 respondents) and employee interviews (125 respondents) to prepare conclusions and recommendations for action by the superintendent and school board. Copies of the preliminary report from the consultants and report writers were sent to Dokens; Marene Casey, district public communications director; Bernie Elston, assistant superintendent for secondary education; Lowena Rogers, assistant superintendent for elementary education; and Art "Red" Bennett, personnel director.

These five members of the superintendent's executive cabinet, after completing their individual reviews of the preliminary report, met to share perceptions and make recommendations for the focus and coverage of the final report. The superintendent opened the session in the administrative conference room.

Dokens: Thanks for assembling promptly. I want all of you to realize that this report is still in draft form. While the factual data and comments will be reported fully and without alteration, the focus and arrangement are open for altering. My major interest this morning, however, is in the implications of findings and conclusions reported in the study. I have definite reactions to some of the suggestions but intend to stay mostly out of the discussion at this point, so that my opinions don't unduly sway your own. That's why I have asked Marene to preside over this strictly advisory session.

Casey: We've all had a couple of days plus a weekend to read through this draft of the Employee Survey Report. Any general reactions first?

Elston: Marene, I understand why Ken asked you to chair this discussion. You're in the business of finding the bright side to publicize and talk about. Frankly, I can't find too many positive things in here. Are we really doing that badly?

Bennett: Don't be such a pessimist, Bernie. I find a lot of good things in this report—things we can be proud about and can feel we're meeting a lot of our educational goals.

Rogers: I agree, Red, but on balance it looks pretty dismal about our relationships with over 3,200 employees. That should have you worried— you're the one who has point contact with all the bargaining groups. Didn't these negative ratings give you nightmares about the next round of negotiations?

Casey: Whoa, everybody. I guess I got what I deserved, asking for general reactions. Before we jump way out ahead of ourselves, what I propose we do is step back and look at the specific data presented here, so we can come to some agreement about what the numbers and the comments are telling us. I suggest we approach it the way the report is arranged, and look first at the "good news." Not so incidentally, Red, I agree that there are positive elements to build upon here. Look on page 4, for example, under "Conclusions—Positive Contributions."

Rogers: What the employees are saying, pretty much across the board— all categories and levels of experience—are these things [reading]:

- I like working for Mountain City Schools.
- I like the kind of work I do.
- I enjoy the people I work with.
- I have a lot to say about how I do my job.

Bennett: Look at the positive ratings on statements about their immediate supervisors:

- My supervisor is responsive to my concerns and suggestions.
- My supervisor deals fairly and openly with me.
- I feel free to disagree with my supervisor.
- My supervisor encourages high performance standards.

Casey: And my favorite area:

- Information is readily available on opportunities for staff development.
- I have enough information to do my job well.
- District (employee) publications are a valuable source of information.

See, these areas are all among the highest rated scores from the written survey, and they are supported by what employees said in their interviews. I'd say those are some strong, positive, baseline attitudes we ought to reinforce and understand as the context for criticism of how we operate. To me, these things say our people like to work here, but, yes, we still have some problems with the way the district operates and treats us as employees.

Dokens: I appreciate your making that point. I too feel as if there are a lot of reasons we can be upbeat about how our employees see Mountain City Schools District as an employer. But...here I go, expressing my reactions when I don't want to do so up front. I admit I was discouraged by some of the low ratings in other areas. I'll be quiet again.

Casey: All right, let's look at the conclusions that our consultants have kindly labeled "Areas for Improvement." What jumps out at us in the most compelling way?

Elston: This is where I admit I was surprised that employees—most of the employees—feel so negative about central administrators at The Hill. That hurts, folks, because that's us!

Rogers: Bernie, I don't see where it is all that deep a distrust. Where are you reading that?

Elston: Look at the tables that report the scores from the survey...on page 37 in Appendix G: All Employees. The next two pages break the results into Certificated and Classified groupings. Just look...very low agreement scores—no, I would call them negative scores on these areas:

- Recognition is given for my efforts toward professional growth.
- My supervisor gives me useful feedback on my potential for advancement.
- I receive frequent informal feedback on how well I am doing my job.
- I trust district administrators. [Look at that! Lowest score on the survey!]
- Mountain City Schools encourage differences of opinion.
- Top management is open and honest in dealing with employees.

And there are others in there about as bad. Hey, it sounds as if we're not doing a very good job of paying attention to our people.

Bennett: I think what impressed me the most—the least?—were the interview comments about lack of input and lack of influence. I agree our employees are giving us a message.

Rogers: What comments are you referring to, Art?

Bennett: Those are in the Appendix, too...I think Appendices J and K. That's where I spent most of my time reviewing the draft copy. For instance—I'm reading on page 45, Appendix J:

- The Hill doesn't make personal visits, so they don't really know what's happening or what is being done.
- Upward communication is not sought, not wanted.

- I have only seen three administrators at this school in my three years here.
- The Hill wants it their way, and you'd better live with that.

Rogers: That is a rather long list, isn't it? [continues reading]

- Decision making is just done and announced, and we just do it.
- Classified personnel need better liaison with management—we feel ignored.
- I feel my input means nothing to MCS.
- We have to beg to get a decision when we've submitted information or requests.

Dokens: I have to say something! In the first place, the people in this room aren't being singled out—at least I don't think so, even though some of the survey and interview comments make it sound that way. I know I have a mandated visit or visits to buildings every week so that I do get to every district location on a regular basis. And you are out into the school sites frequently—maybe not Art, but the rest of you are. No, I don't think we're the ones not getting out; it's the rest of the people in this building.

Casey: But Ken, they're also saying when we visit or when we solicit information, we aren't really listening or considering what they say. Plus, we don't do a very good job even acknowledging that they said anything.

Dokens: That may well be true…If so, we're the ones who will have to make some changes. I read the primary recommendation in this report, however, and I have to admit the data supports—overwhelmingly—that recommendation: "The Hill needs to get in touch with the people in the front lines." That won't happen by expecting or even mandating that employees come to us. It will have to be the other way around.

Elston: I can tell you right now there will be a battle to implement anything that adds traveling out to the trenches.

Bennett: I'll second that. The last round of downsizing cut central administrative positions almost exclusively. I know lots of employees, though, as well as many in the public, who still feel we are top-heavy administratively. Just last week I asked one of our Title III supervisors to visit two elementary schools. She turned, looked me in the eye, and said, "I'll put it to you straight. Do you want me to make the visits, or do you want the district in trouble because we did not turn in our federal, state, and community reports on time?" I didn't push the matter any further.

Dokens: I understand that. I know people here are carrying heavy, even extra, loads since the reduction. Just the same, when this report is finalized and accepted by the board, when it is made available—as we promised—to the media and to the employee groups, there will be a howling to implement that major recommendation. We have a little lead time, but not much. Better be brainstorming now because we will be doing something!

CASE 4

PART B. SEVERAL YEARS LATER
Gary L. Peterson

Superintendent Marcus Lansing swiveled his desk chair around to greet Leslie Tingey, Mountain City Schools' experienced director of communications, as she arrived for their weekly Monday 8:00 A.M. overview. "Well, Leslie, it appears we've done it again. The troops clearly have low morale, and many of our administrative managers do not understand why—or even believe the results of our latest employee survey. I've already had some calls from members of our management team wondering who or what our employees are talking about. Did you finish your copy of the report over the weekend?"

Tingey: I've not only read it; I've highlighted pages and sections, written in the margins, and I'm already concerned about how we can prepare a positive sounding summary. I am not surprised by the findings, however.

Lansing: You know, I have to admit that I am more than a bit discouraged. Neither you nor I have been here longer than two years, and it is evident that many of these very same attitudes existed well before we arrived. I knew coming in that there was a residue of unhappiness in the ranks. There have been two—actually three—short-term superintendents since [Kenneth] Dokens left, and the cuts and some new programs were not well accepted. I did feel, however, that in the recent past employees felt more included and listened to.

Tingey: Well, I'm discouraged, too, but not by the findings. We felt it was time to redo this survey with staff; we asked the questions, and were they ever ready to give us their opinions! Look, over half of the employees wrote notes on the survey or even attached extra pages. No, this we asked for and now we need to pay attention to them.

Lansing: How long has it been since that first comprehensive survey?

Tingey: About ten years now. Did you see how closely the survey response numbers correlated to those taken on the same questions years ago?

Lansing: Well, it seems the staff consistently have told us that they have high job satisfaction in a lot of ways: they like their work, the people they work with, their immediate supervisors, and they way their supervisors treat them. Just as consistently, they are dissatisfied with a lack of upward communication, with too little real involvement and participation. They want accessibility and meaningful visits—still!

Tingey: And those programs and recent policy changes we have been touting—they have not been well received because they are not uniformly applied, or because they are seen as just another edict coming from the Hill. The LDM [location decision making] was instituted at least partly because that placed more choices and decisions at the local sites, where they told us they wanted more say. The Secondary staff and the Certificated employees in particular rated administrative trust and honesty low. Their ratings were lower on 90 percent of the survey questions.

Lansing: Well, those numbers are rather convincing—again. I'm a believer, but here are some of our central administrators saying to me that they do not know specifically what kinds of things are causing the greatest difficulty. You are the professional, Leslie; tell me, how are we going to provide additional evidence and convince all our colleagues we refer to as administrative personnel that this touches all of us and that we have to address the widespread dissatisfaction and low morale?

QUESTIONS FOR DISCUSSION

1. Based on information from the Employee Survey Report, what assumptions might you make about overall school district employee morale? How do you justify those assumptions?
2. How do you account for the generally positive attitudes toward immediate supervisors and the generally negative feelings toward top administrators? How might the district capitalize on the positive to work on the negative?
3. In this organization there generally was satisfaction with the administration as a source of important and necessary information. How does that satisfaction affect attitudes with upward communication?
4. It indeed appears that Mountain City Schools employees have changed little in the things they both like and dislike about working for the school district. With such long-term dissatisfaction, what will it take to change those attitudes?
5. If you were Lansing and Tingey, what steps would you take to convince other administrative officers that the problem must be seriously and significantly addressed? Then, assuming more widespread concurrence, what would you do?

SELECTED BIBLIOGRAPHY

Downs, C. W., & Hazen, M. D. (1977). A factor analytic study of communication satisfaction. *Journal of Business Communication, 14*(3), 63–73.

Jablin, F. (1980). Organizational communication theory and research: An overview of communication climate and network research. In D. Nimmo (Ed.), *Communication Yearbook* (Vol. 4, 327–347). New Brunswick, NJ: Transaction-International Communication Association.

James, L. R., & Jones, A. P. (1974). Organizational climate: A review of theory and research. *Psychological Bulletin, 81,* 1096–1112.

Schneider, B., & Bartlett, C. J. (1968). Individual differences and organizational climate. *Personnel Psychology, 21,* 323–333.

Waters, L. K., Roach, D., & Batlis, N. (1974). Organizational climate dimensions and job-related attitudes. *Personnel Psychology, 27,* 465–476.

Wiio, O. (1977). Organizational communication: Interfacing systems. *Finnish Journal of Business Economics* (special edition), *2,* 259–285.

Managing Information Flow

CHARLES CORPORATION

Jillian Pierson and Deborah Jaeger

BACKGROUND

Charles Corporation is a multinational organization with headquarters in the eastern United States, offices throughout the country, and subsidiaries in Asia and Europe. The company places a strong emphasis on continuous quality improvement and customer satisfaction. Its annual publications clearly delineate cultural values and expected behaviors from all organizational members.

One of the company's western U.S. divisions was preparing to get to work on an offshore product development project that would eventually involve at least five sites in four countries. In addition to the western U.S. site, two of the locations were subsidiaries of Charles Corporation; the others were subcontractors. The project was expected to last eighteen months. The product in development was critical to the future of the entire organization and was based on a newly developed technology that required new learning from all project members. Charles Corporation said it was going offshore because the skills needed were not available at home and because the company wanted the advantages of research grant support in other countries. Because the company anticipated peaks and valleys in the amount of work needed, it also wanted to use offshore subcontractors and subsidiaries.

Current communication in the organization relied heavily on electronic mail transmitted via CharlesCorp's private network. Subcontractors were not on the system and had to use faxes. The company had tried some teleconferencing and was considering the purchase of a new videoconferencing system. Time differences were an obvious factor; several managers spoke to offshore members from home in early morning or late evening.

The primary subsidiary management involved was located in Singapore, a country with a multicultural history, where the population is made up of approximately 77 percent Chinese, 15 percent Malay, and 7 percent Indian. The British legacy remains, and there is a high level of proficiency in English, the official language of education and commerce. Dubbed the "intelligent island," Singapore has manufacturing facilities of over 650 multinational corporations (Sisodia, 1992) and has made an effort to learn from more developed countries (Choy, 1987). The government has waged a national campaign since 1982 to bolster productivity, which may make the culture particularly open to foreign management styles (Check-Teck, 1992). Traditional, family-style Chinese management was a major influence but could never be adopted fully in Singapore because of the British administration. Choy (1987) argues that the various pressures and proximity of different communities living on the one island has led to a very "culturally fluid" society. For Singapore this has meant that "the boundaries of the cultural universe are often ill-defined, and are characterized by the existence of overlapping and even possibly conflicting norms and values which are tolerated and can be considered acceptable so long as the resulting courses of actions achieve socially desirable results" (p. 134).

Charles Corporation (CharlesCorp) was concerned about preventing communication and coordination problems in this project, which was a new form of operation for them. A group of engineers from the Singapore subsidiary was invited to the western U.S. division for an eight-week training period. Several members of CharlesCorp's organizational development department were asked to participate in learning how the selected project team members viewed the anticipated differences and challenges in communication. The research team was composed of project director Karin Tenney, Ben Webster, and Chi-Lu Jin, who agreed to distribute a written questionnaire and conduct interviews with individual members of the global team.

ASSESSING THE RESULTS

The data-collecting phase of the project was complete. Tenney had set up this meeting in one of CharlesCorp's conference rooms. The research team's goals were prominently displayed on one of the white board surfaces:

Question 1a: Which channels did employees favor for complex messages?
Question 1b: Which channels did employees favor for routine messages?

Question 2: Do employees perceive that the information they get from team members in the same location is more timely than information they receive from overseas members?

Question 3: Is there a difference in channel preference between the cultures?

Flanking those questions were two large-print questions: "What did we discover, and so what?" and "What does Charles Corporation want to know and need to know?"

Tenney: Here we are. This is the point we have been aiming for, to have all the data together for us to do the "making-sense" work. With our purposes and questions right before us, what did we in fact obtain?

Webster: I have tabulated and run the questionnaire results. I know we were disappointed in the return rate from our sample. I do think that it is an accurate reflection of perceptions; however, I am not pleased with less than a 50 percent return from what we've agreed is a potentially biased sample because the subjects were selected by the company.

Tenney: Let's hear your findings, and we'll see if we can justify conclusions from them. Remember, we have valuable interview data which might verify or invalidate what they told us on your written questionnaire.

Webster: OK. Here is what I have from twenty-one persons—eight from Singapore, the balance from the western U.S. office. For our first question on channel preference: For simple messages, the single greatest preference was for E-mail (47.6 percent); for difficult-to-interpret, nonroutine (ambiguous) messages, 81 percent prefer face-to-face communication.

Tenney: How about the timeliness question?

Webster: We developed mean scores for the various sources of information used by team members. Overall, the mean scores on a 5-point Likert scale read like this: for immediate supervisors, 3.25; for managers, 3.11; for coworkers, same location, 3.10; for overseas team members, 3.06; and for senior staff, 2.84.

Tenney: There is not really much distinction among those ratings— certainly not much difference in timeliness of messages from overseas sources.

Webster: The next question on channel preference by cultural areas provides what I find to be interesting perceptions.

Jin: How so, Ben?

Webster: Well, the Singapore group rated E-mail as more preferable than did the U.S. group and face-to-face as less preferable than the U.S. respondents.

Jin: Why are you surprised at this finding?

Webster: On the face value of these expressed preferences, this seems to contradict what we have assumed about nearly all Asian, high-context cultures. Until you report what you discovered from the interviews, this is not what I would have expected to find.

Tenney: All right, then, unless you have other telling points from the questionnaires? No? Then let's explore what Chi-Lu and I have summarized from our interviews. Remember, this group is only about half the size of your returned questionnaire sample but includes an acceptable representation across positions and from both locations.

Jin: Remember too, that these were exploratory interviews, which helped us frame the questions for the survey as well as provided us with broader perceptions about communicating across channels, teams, and time zones.

Tenney: First of all, every global team member we interviewed identified communication as their major challenge facing the alliance for this project. They worried about several things:

- Message clarity
- The ability of information technology to help provide mutual understanding of what promised to be—in many instances—technical material
- Time pressures to complete the project, and even phases of the project
- Constant need for task clarification
- A constantly evolving agenda and schedule
- Need to coordinate their efforts across several countries

In our interviews, the employees expressed preferences for the use of one channel over another, depending upon the task at hand. This finding generally parallels what Ben has conveyed to us about questionnaire responses. They further volunteered that:

- E-mail is useful because it is cost-efficient;
- E-mail (or other asynchronous communication methods) are useful because of the time allowed to react and to leave a written record of those reactions;
- E-mail has weaknesses as well: difficulty in communicating certain kinds of information; the need to rephrase questions several times; the need to ask for verbal (oral) clarification *after* receiving E-mails.

Webster: You asked specifically about teleconferences, too. What were the attitudes?

Jin: Teleconferencing was perceived as particularly useful for decision making. However, such a channel is not seen as having the ability to be specific about high-level technical information. In addition, they sensed they would have a high need to accommodate to difficult time zone differences.

Webster: How about the lack of nonverbal communication present in teleconferences?

Jin: These managers and engineers felt that limitation did not constitute an obstacle to transfer of technical information but that it does impede decision making. A number of the employees brought up the need to use more direct statements than when they could communicate face-to-face.

One project manager—who had previous experience with synchronous computer mediated communication (CMC) elsewhere—said he preferred that to telephone conversations, where an individual's vocal characteristics could actually be a hindrance. Most workers—across the locations—agreed that face-to-face meetings are a necessity, especially for coordinating the work of various groups.

Webster: In the interviews you probed for concerns about intercultural challenges. What did they tell you?

Tenney: Several of our interviewees answered that they were completely unconcerned about intercultural problems. One of the global managers expressed it this way: "Miscommunication may happen in initial interactions, but after several months of working with [someone from] a new culture, such problems disappear because the code of a 'foreigner' is then understood." Actually, the only adjustments any of our interviewees mentioned making for overseas partners were in the area of setting clear expectations because so many were new to Charles Corporation.

One of the managers emphasized the need for communication to make certain that the offshore members felt part of the team. He said he gave information they didn't necessarily need just to give them a sense of belonging. He also said it was critical to listen to new partners' input in planning stages and to endeavor to incorporate at least some those ideas.

Webster: Weren't there any complaints or concerns at all about intercultural issues?

Jin: We did hear complaints from the Americans that Singaporeans have a tendency to only deliver exactly what they've been asked to do. That can create problems when U.S. managers expect more proactive contributions. Another concern voiced was the importance of using very precise messages when dealing with their advanced technology. One of the reasons for their extensive training period was to develop and to agree very specifically on what terminology to use. The Singapore project manager, an Indian national, mentioned difficulties created when a software architect had not participated in any group decision making nor had messages checked by other team members for clarity. However, most of the problems cited were about individual habits or failings—not something which could be cited as cultural differences.

Tenney: There really are a few surprises in all this data. Can we draw at least some tentative conclusions from the findings of both of our data-gathering instruments?

Webster: Well, while there are clear preferences about channels to use for certain types of messages, I do not think we can determine cultural differences as a factor. I do find it interesting, and promising also, that messages from overseas were seen as timely as the messages from coworkers in the same location. In addition, I am surprised that it was not the Singaporeans who most favored face-to-face communication.

Jin: Ben, I really think the Americans on this project relied less on E-mail in their ordinary course of business. Despite the value expressed about CMC, project members still see a need for regular face-to-face sessions. The Asian emphasis on developing trust prior to entering a business relationship may partially explain the ongoing need for the face-to-face interactions, especially when CMC is essentially devoid of socioemotional content.

Tenney: I really think the complaint that Singapore team members don't work proactively may be due to their views on authority and role boundaries.

Jin: Also, being extremely direct may be difficult for those from high-context cultures.

Webster: Sounds to me like you are saying there are in fact intercultural factors at work here. Why then did most of your subjects not express any intercultural concerns?

Jin: I'm not at all sure. These are highly qualified and capable people in this organization, and they came across as clearly optimistic and confident. It seems likely too that the participants' professional culture as engineers gave them so much in common that those commonalties outweighed their national culture differences. Perhaps their perceptions also might reflect a lack of awareness of cultural assumptions which they will find underscoring their shared activities.

Tenney: You know, what I would be interested in exploring further in our company is the interesting mix of cultures already within both the U.S. and the Singapore teams. The U.S. team for this project has Japanese, African American, and [East] Indian members. Several Singapore members were of Indian, not Chinese, descent. Could it be also that Singapore is really that different than many cultural expectations we have tended to label as Asian? Could these elements explain the cultural issues and complications we have identified?

Jin: I certainly want to learn more, as I think the folks upstairs will want to as well. What happens to informal processes and trust building in global alliances such as these?

Webster: Hey, slow down. There are other implications for us and for the company in all these findings—limited as they are. I think we are sufficiently clear on what our conclusions should look like. Let's get to work preparing statements and questions to the company. That is what they are paying us to do.

QUESTIONS FOR DISCUSSION

1. Do the findings of this group of corporate investigators confirm that while multicultural work teams may benefit from a wider range of perspectives and less "groupthink," they may have to struggle against the potential barriers of mistrust, miscommunication, and stress?
2. To what extent are organization and culture bound together?
3. Why is adaptation so necessary to suit the assumptions of the expanding contexts of multinational organizations?
4. How do you anticipate that future information technology changes will impact the way communication takes place in intercultural exchanges?
5. It has been argued that E-mail contributes to the breakdown of organizations' hierarchies. Did it appear to do so for this project in the Charles Corporation?

REFERENCES

Check-Teck, F. (1992). Culture, productivity and structure: A Singapore study. *Organization Studies, 13,* 589–609.
Choy, C. L. (1987). History and managerial culture in Singapore: "Pragmatism," "openness" and "paternalism." *Asia Pacific Journal of Management, 4,* 133–143.
Sisodia, R. S. (1992). Singapore invests in the nation-corporation. *Harvard Business Review, 70,* 40–50.

SELECTED BIBLIOGRAPHY

Adler, N. J. (1991). *International dimensions of organizational behavior* (2nd ed.). Boston: PWS-Kent.
DiBella, A. J. (1993). The role of assumptions in implementing management practices across cultural boundaries. *Journal of Applied Behavioral Science, 29,* 311–327.

Ghoshal, S., Korine, H., & Szulanski, G. (1994). Interunit communication in multinational corporations. *Management Science, 40,* 96–110.

Hofstede, G. (1980). *Culture's consequences: International differences in work-related values.* Beverly Hills, CA: Sage.

Maddox, R. C. (1993). *Cross-cultural problems in international business.* Westport, CT: Quorum.

Parkhe, A. (1991). Interfirm diversity, organizational learning, and longevity in global strategic alliances. *Journal of International Business Studies, 22*(4), 579–601.

Roche, E. M. (1986). *Managing information technology in multinational corporations.* New York: Macmillan.

Trevino, L. K., Lengel, R. H., & Daft, R. L. (1987). Media symbolism, media richness, and media choice in organizations. *Communication Research, 14,* 553–574.

Yoon, J. O. (1988). The impact of Confucianism on interpersonal relationships and communication patterns in East Asia. *Communication Monographs, 55,* 374–389.

CASE **6**

KCCB'S MISSING MASTERPIECE
Scott Hammond

At ten minutes before 9:00 P.M. on a Friday night, KCCB program director Ann Howard was at home, sitting down to watch the first locally produced news documentary on her station when the telephone rang. "This is John, in master control, calling. We can't find the tape of the news special that's supposed to air in ten minutes. What should we do?" Howard quickly gave instructions for a backup program to the master control operator. With nine minutes before air time, she began making telephone calls to locate the tape. She didn't expect to find the key people at home on Friday night and she was right. At two minutes to 9:00 P.M. she gave up her phone calls, got into her car, and went down to the station. For the next two hours she took phone calls from angry viewers complaining about the last-minute change in television programs.

KCCB is one of three commercial television stations in a medium-sized midwestern city. The station had a reputation for having a strong commitment to local programming and news. The 6:00 P.M. and 10:00 P.M. news programs had a long tradition of quality, and until a year ago, had the same number of viewers as both of the other news stations combined. Because of KCCB's success, its commercial time sold at a higher rate. News was very profitable for the station. In fact, it was so profitable that the station had enjoyed an average growth in revenue of 23.4 percent for the last five years.

In the past year another local commercial station had begun increasing its coverage of local news and had picked up in the ratings. KCCB was still the front-runner but was losing ground. Since neither of the other stations was producing news documentaries on a regular basis, station management felt that this would be a good way to recapture a larger share of the news audience.

What KCCB management decided to do was to produce a documentary called "Daddy, I Want to Play Football." The station's senior sports reporter followed an eighteen-year-old cancer victim, trying to make good his dream of playing football for a well-known high school team. The documentary was full of irony and emotion. Some people in the news department thought it would win national awards. The promotion department waited until a week before the air date to promote the documentary so as not to give the other stations time to react with counterprogramming. Then KCCB began a promotion blitz, running two spots every hour on the air and buying advertising space in local newspapers as well as time on radio stations. Station manager Bob Gibson and news director Roy Hart were particularly proud of the documentary and the promotion effort. They called it a "masterpiece."

Hart was quoted as saying that, "the cost of production and promotion was almost twice the amount of revenue that the documentary is able to generate, but airing the show is expected to boost the morale of the people in the news department and at the station. The main purpose is directed at the public. Hopefully this program alone will help establish KCCB once again as the station most committed to news."

Station manager Bob Gibson was reluctant to approve this type of expensive effort at first but turned out to be very supportive. "When Roy came to me with the idea for the documentary, yes, I was reluctant. Then I saw the May book [news ratings]. The documentary seemed like a way to dig us out of a hole and get us back in front in the news game. At the rate we were dropping, the guys across town would have caught up with us in two years. That would cut our ad revenue in half."

The big point was that KCCB made almost half of its revenue selling commercial time during the local news. The second big money-maker was sports production, because KCCB owned the broadcast rights to a National Basketball Association (NBA®) professional team. The station typically broadcast between twenty and thirty games a year, as well as some of the basketball and football games of a local university. These two activities accounted for another large share of ad revenue. Jack Hawkins, sports producer for KCCB, always worked the professional games when the network came to town to broadcast NBA® play. Because Hawkins had a reputation for being the best sports producer in the market, he was selected to do this special, even though it was his first documentary. His lack of experience in documentary production didn't seem to concern anyone.

News director Hart said, "Jack is by far one of the best in the business. We are lucky to have him around here. But having a good employee like that means you have to find him new challenges. We have some producers in the news department who would have liked to try this thing. But I just couldn't say 'no' when Jack came over from production and asked to be involved."

Jack Hawkins was not part of the news or of the sports department. He was a producer/director in the production department. When he failed to see the documentary on which he had worked so hard make it on the air, he first called Roy Hart, then he tried to call Ann Howard. At midnight, when Hawkins finally got through to Howard, tempers flared.

Hawkins: A month's work, a week's promotion, and your people can't even get my show on the air.

Howard: Jack, before you blame anyone, I want you to tell me what you know.

Hawkins: What happened? I spend a month busting my butt on this stupid thing, including spending the last forty-eight hours straight putting the finishing touches on it in the editing room, and your people can't even find the tape.

Howard: I found the tape. It was on Bill Jay's desk. What was it doing there?

Hawkins: That's where I delivered it!

Howard: What good does that do? If the traffic department doesn't have your tape, then how do you expect to get it on the air?

Hawkins: My job is producing the show. Traffic's job is getting it on the air. I'm a producer, not your gopher. [And with that pronouncement, Jack hung up.]

THE DAY AFTER

Ann Howard reached the office early. As she had expected, within a few minutes she was in a meeting with Bob Gibson. Howard had worked for Gibson for almost ten years. Their families sometimes vacationed together. Howard always felt as if she had an ally in Gibson. She knew he would be angry about the situation with the documentary, but she hoped this would be the crisis that brought about some change.

Gibson was in his office thinking about the situation. He knew that Jack Hawkins operated under few constraints. He was given a project, assigned resources, and was expected to produce a program worthy of broadcast. His creativity was essential and, according to his associates, an intrinsic resource for the organization. Over a beer once, Hawkins had told Gibson that organizational constraints were "useless bureaucracy." Most of the managers thought that Jack's creativity would be stifled if they put more restraints on him. They were willing to put up with his idiosyncrasies for "the good of the organization."

Susan, in traffic, on the other hand, worked under tight constraints. She was always told which programs to broadcast when. Her job was one of high structure and few choices.

When Howard entered the room, Gibson, in his "neutral" voice said, "Ann, that was a major screwup. The station owners are mad. The switchboard is still flooded with calls from angry viewers. Last night I even got a call at home from Jack Hawkins telling me I should fire someone. What happened?"

Howard had always respected Gibson's professionalism. She knew that his "neutral voice" was as mad as he ever got in public. She also knew that the anger was not directed at her. "As you know," she explained, "all the tapes in master control, all our programs, are set up by the traffic department. Susan is in charge of getting the right program at the right place at the right time. The master control operators are too busy running the air signal to worry about where the next show is coming from. The promotion department, the advertising department, news, and production are all responsible to get their tapes to Susan. She can't go looking for everything. As near as I can tell, last night the production department didn't get the show over to traffic. I found the tape on the production manager's desk."

Gibson countered, "Jack says he delivered the tape to Bill Jay." Howard explained that the system was more complex than just dropping a tape on someone's desk. "Bob, you know it is the producer's responsibility to deliver all tapes to Susan. She doesn't have the time to go looking for all the tapes. But yesterday, she did go looking for Jack to get the show ready for air. When she couldn't find him, she told Bill Jay she needed the tape. Bill promised he would deliver the tape to master control. When Bill talked to Jack, the show was still being edited. Bill says he told Jack to take the show to master control. Jack says he was told to put it on Jay's desk. Either way, it didn't make it on the air."

Gibson and Howard then went down to see Bill Jay about the situation. He was fresh from having his ear bent by an angry Jack Hawkins, who was threatening to quit if heads didn't roll. Even so, Jay was honest and forthright, and had what they thought was telling insight into the problem. "When you gave me this job a year ago, I thought it was a promotion becoming a manager. Instead, I'm just a gopher. You gave me the production manager's job because I was an engineer, not a producer. I knew how to schedule the equipment and knew technical limitations. But these guys that work for me are in a different world. They are creative types—so creative that they hardly work an eight-hour day sometimes, and other times I can't get them to go home. Take Jack. He does what he wants. He has been producing for fifteen years, and you want to keep him producing. He doesn't let me tell him what to do. He knows I can't fire him. He knows I don't sign the paychecks. In fact, he makes more money freelancing for the network for four weeks during football season than he does in a year at this place. The only reason he stays around is for the benefits and to fulfill his life-long mission of giving me a hard time."

In a direct way Gibson asked, "What caused this problem yesterday?" Jay's response was less direct: "Well, part of the problem is that the producers work over in the annex most of the time. When they're not there, they're on the road doing sports or out with a commercial client. Except for their contact with me, they have almost no contact with anyone else at the station. They work in a separate place and do different things. They control their own productions, work their own hours, and even have their own budgets. All I do is see that the equipment is working and that they don't schedule the same camera for two different locations. The other day I got a call from the promotion department. They said one producer had sent them a bill for producing a promotion for our air. When challenged, the producer said: "We have to make money, too."

Gibson listened for a while and then asked Bill to get to the point. "What about last night's show?" Jay replied, "This girl—I think her name was Susan—came by looking for Jack. He was still editing and the show was only four hours from air so I told her I would tell him to get her the tape. I found Jack and said, 'Be sure to take care of your tape.' He thought that meant put it on my desk. So when I got to work this morning, here it was."

Howard and Gibson left Jay's office, wondering how they would explain the situation to the station owners. They knew that producing the documentary had been a risky and costly high-level decision. They knew that they would need a good explanation of what happened and a good plan to keep it from happening again.

QUESTIONS FOR DISCUSSION

1. Is the problem in this case related to the formal or the informal organization? Who was formally responsible for the mix-up? Would a change in the structure of the organization keep the problem from happening again?
2. Would you describe the organization at KCCB as loosely or tightly coupled? Is that good or bad? What effect does the organizational structure have on the constraints or on the agency of individuals?
3. Conduct a decision and relations analysis as suggested by Peter Drucker. (Drucker, P. J. [1977]. *People and performance: The best of Peter Drucker on management.* New York: Harper & Row.) What changes, if any, would you make?

4. To what extent are issues of integration and differentiation helpful in understanding this case?
5. Do a network analysis for each key player in the organization. Where does information flow overlap for each key player? How is information transmitted in the organization? How would you remedy this situation?
6. Propose a solution.

SELECTED BIBLIOGRAPHY

Greenbaum, H., Hellweg, S. A., & Falcione, R. L. (1988). Organizational communication evaluation: An overview 1950–1981. In G. M. Goldhaber & G. A. Barnett (Eds.), *Handbook of organizational communication* (pp. 275–317). Norwood, NJ: Ablex.

Lawrence, P. R., & Lorsch, J. W. (1967). *Organization and environment managing differentiation and integration.* Boston: Division of Research Graduate School of Business Administration.

Pace, R. W., Peterson, B. D., & Boren, R. R. (1975). *Communication experiments: A manual for conducting experiments* (pp. 171–188). Belmont, CA: Wadsworth.

CASE **7**

WHEN CULTURES COLLIDE

Staff Participation in Hiring an Executive

Nina Gregg

BACKGROUND INFORMATION

The HELP (Heal, Educate, Learn, Prevent) Center is a twenty-five-year-old regional not-for-profit organization in the southeastern United States. The organization's mission is "to lessen the trauma of sexual assault and to reduce the incidence of sexual assault" through crisis intervention, counseling, education, and prevention. All services provided by the center, which has seventeen employees (ten full-time-equivalent) and a pool of trained volunteers, are free of charge. These services include a twenty-four-hour help line, legal advocacy, individual and group therapy, hospital accompaniment, in-school programs, community education, and training events for professional service providers. The center has an excellent reputation throughout its eight-county service region and among law enforcement, social service, health care providers, and school personnel, as well as among its clients. Its annual budget of nearly $500,000 comes from contributions from individuals, fundraising events, foundation and corporate grants, the United Way, and grants from local municipalities and state and federal agencies.

Like similar organizations throughout North America, the HELP Center was founded in the early 1970s as an all-volunteer feminist rape crisis network. As the center has grown and as its funding base has developed, it has taken on more of the structural characteristics of a conventional social service agency, while maintaining a commitment to feminist values in relationships among staff and in the orientation of programs and program content. These two features of the HELP Center—a conventional structure and a participatory work culture—came into conflict recently when the organization launched a search for a new executive director.

The organization's structure has the appearance of a traditional hierarchy, with a board of directors, an executive director, four program coordinators, and various staff positions. The fourteen-member board of directors is composed of area professionals such as attorneys, managers, accountants, and leaders in other area agencies. The board meets monthly to conduct routine business and relies heavily on the executive director for reports regarding program developments, staff performance, and the status of the budget. Board members have met all the center staff at least once, but they interact regularly only with the executive director. About half the board members are approaching or have passed the statutory limit of their terms of service. The remaining board members have joined the board within the past year or two.

The center's staff, although holding conventional job titles, engage in everyday practices that are inclusive, cooperative, and participatory. Program and policy decisions are undertaken in a consultative process, and many job duties overlap and are shared. This environment is responsible for the low turnover among HELP Center staff, who work long hours (including twenty-four-hour shifts on call), for less-than-competitive wages, in positions that require compassion, understanding, and sensitivity in the daily presence of violence and abuse. The current executive director has been in this position for over ten years. The average length of service among center staff is over seven years.

THE SITUATION

In July the HELP Center's executive director, Louise Antrobus, announced her intention to step down from her leadership position, with a target date for her departure of four to six months. This announcement sent shock waves throughout the organization. In the break room staff shared their reactions. "Louise hired me right out of college; she taught me everything I know," recalled one senior staff member. "She hired *all* of us," another staff member reminded everyone. Others wondered about the center's credibility under a new executive director, for Antrobus's long association with the organization and her receipt of a service award from the local chapter of the National Conference contributed to the center's positive public image.

The president of the board of directors, Anita Webster, was similarly affected by Antrobus's announcement. Antrobus met Webster for lunch to give advance notice. Upon hearing the news, Webster exclaimed, "I hope you are going to help us find your replacement!" That evening, Antrobus formally presented her resignation to the board. "What do we do now?" a newer board member asked. "You will need to form a Search Committee," Antrobus advised, and she redirected further questions about the search process to the board's Executive Committee. "We are going to need your help," stated the board's vice president. "You will have to write a job description, because we really don't know what you do." In response, Webster reminded the board of its role: "This is our responsibility, not Louise's, and I am sure we can manage it together." The meeting was adjourned, without beginning the task of searching for a new executive director.

About six weeks after Antrobus announced her plans, the board began developing a Search Committee. In accordance with the center's bylaws, the committee was composed of board members who volunteered and were approved by the board's Executive Committee. The search procedure called for the Search Committee to conduct the search and present likely candidates to the entire board. The board's Executive Committee was empowered, by the bylaws, to make the final hiring decision.

Three of the five Search Committee members had been on the board for several years: Phil Solway, a local attorney, was the immediate past president of the board; Lindsay Farkus, a former travel agent, could always be counted on to do the board work no one else wanted to do; and Anita Webster, current board president and manager of another local agency serving women. Marjorie Reed, a manager of a local telecommunications company, and Angela Lechter, minister to a local church congregation, were newer board members who volunteered to join the Search Committee. Lechter also volunteered to chair the committee.

Under Lechter's guidance, the Search Committee began developing a job description and a position announcement. Both were based on the Search Committee's experience working with Antrobus and their expectation that a new executive director would have her skills as well as some additional expertise to address changes in the organization. About two months after Antrobus's announcement, the Search Committee placed the position announcement in area newspapers and mailed out flyers announcing the search.

Anticipating the approach of Antrobus's desired departure in November, at the end of August HELP Center staff began wondering what was going on with the search. At the close of a weekly staff meeting, the designated spokesperson asked, "Louise, what is the status of the search? We haven't heard anything from you or from the board." Antrobus referred that question and all staff inquiries to the Search Committee. In the hallway after the meeting, three senior staff discussed strategy. "I think we need to contact the Search Committee and ask them what is going on," said one. "I want more than information," said another; "I want to participate in the process, like we do in all our internal decision making." The three decided to poll the staff and gauge support for a group inquiry to the board. With the support secure, staff members composed a letter to the board of directors. In the letter, the staff expressed their interest in and their desire to participate in the search process. The staff invited the Search Committee to a September staff meeting "to discuss together our inclusion in the search process."

The Search Committee responded immediately with a faxed letter addressed to "The HELP Center Staff" and from "The Search Committee." The letter thanked everyone for their concern and offer of assistance, adding that as many committee members as were available would attend the September staff meeting. Appended to the faxed letter was a questionnaire the Search Committee asked each staff member to complete to aid them in the search. The questionnaire asked staff to identify program areas the new executive director would be expected to oversee.

Three members of the Search Committee—Webster, Lechter, and Farkus—attended the September staff meeting. The meeting took place at the center in the executive director's office, which was also the room used for staff meetings. Nearly every staff member (except Antrobus) was present. The room was crowded with bodies, and two of the Search Committee members as well as several staff sat on the floor. Miriam Lennox, a nine-year veteran staff member, suggested opening the meeting with self-introductions. As each staff member spoke, the collective experience in the room made an impression on Lechter. "I did not know there was such widespread lengthy service on this staff," she noted.

The discussion soon turned to defining what the staff meant by "inclusion" in the search process. The conversation was lively, with many staff members contributing. Wendy Paxton, a program coordinator who had worked at the center for four years, described the center's participatory work culture: "We work together more as colleagues than as supervisors and staff. So even though executive searches in other organizations typically do not involve staff, the center is not a traditional organization." Nan Wise, another program coordinator who had been with the center for five years, explained further. "We use a consensus process for all internal hiring, and so we would like to see those values incorporated into this search, too." Leah Rathke, a former intern who had recently been hired into a staff position, impatiently changed the subject: "But what *is* going on with the search? Has it begun?"

Webster appeared relieved as she explained how the Search Committee had been constituted and said, "Yes, the search has begun. We are advertising and circulating a position announcement." "All of you can help us," Farkus quickly added. "You can contribute to the search by circulating the position announcement, informing the Search Committee of characteristics and qualities you would like to see in a new executive director, and giving us sample questions we can ask during candidate interviews." "And," Webster said, "you can complete the questionnaire the Search Committee faxed to you last week."

Lennox attempted to shift the conversation back to what the staff meant by "inclusion" in the search. "In addition to providing you with information," she said, "we would like to participate actively in the search. Would the board be open to this?" "What do you mean?" asked Webster. Lennox hesitated. "We could participate on the Search Committee." "What does that mean?" Webster asked again. "Well, that could mean several things," Paxton offered. "Staff could have equal representation [parity] with board members on the Search Committee; staff could have two or three representatives on the Search Committee; staff could review applications and participate formally in the interviews of candidates."

After a brief silence, Webster took the next step: "I would support bringing to the board a proposal to add two staff members, selected by the staff, to the Search Committee. Angela, you are the Search Committee chair—do you agree?" Lechter nodded, and Webster turned to Farkus, who said, "I think this would be a good solution. We would benefit from the staff input and be able to spread out the work of the Search Committee."

The meeting had gone on for more than an hour, and people were showing signs of needing to get back to work. Finally, Lechter broached the subject that had yet to be named: "Does the staff have confidence in the board to make this decision?" she asked. Without hesitation, Lennox replied, "No. We don't know you and you don't know us." With the trust issue out in the open, the tension in the room mounted, and after a few remarks about maintaining communication between and among the staff and the board, the meeting was adjourned.

QUESTIONS FOR DISCUSSION

1. What do you think are the underlying causes of conflict between the staff and the board?
2. How have communication practices contributed to or eased the conflict?
3. How can the staff and board begin developing trusting relationships?
4. What recommendations would you make to the board and the Search Committee so that this current search satisfies both board and staff members?
5. What more would you like to know before making recommendations regarding communication, participation, and decision making in future searches?
6. What recommendations would you make to the board and staff regarding the organizational issues that emerged during the search?

SELECTED BIBLIOGRAPHY

Cheney, G. (1995). Democracy in the workplace: Theory and practice from the perspective of communication. *Journal of Applied Communication Research, 23,* 167–200.

Ianello, K. P. (1992). *Decisions without hierarchy: Feminist interventions in organization theory and practice.* New York: Routledge.

Kleinman, S. (1996). *Opposing ambitions: Gender and identity in an alternative organization.* Chicago: University of Chicago Press.

Seibold, D. S., & Shea, B. C. (in press). Participation and decision making. In F. M. Jablin & L. L. Putnam (Eds.), *The new handbook of organizational communication.* Thousand Oaks, CA: Sage.

CASE 8

CHANGES AT METROPOLITAN HOSPITAL

Beverly Burke and R. Jeffrey Ringer

Metropolitan Hospital is located in a small midwestern town. The Mental Health Unit (MHU) of the hospital consists of forty-five beds and is staffed with fifteen registered nurses, fifteen nurse aides, and fifteen orderlies. Rebecca Kurbing was hired by Metropolitan as an RN after having worked in the Veterans Hospital Psychiatric Unit. Soon after beginning her new job, Kurbing noticed that the relationship that existed between staff and administration was less than cordial.

There were two positions of authority: head nurse and supervisor. Ardean Kelsey—the head nurse—was a strong, middle-aged woman. Her most notable characteristics were her stern facial expressions and tightly pursed lips. She spoke directly and authoritatively and usually only when something was wrong. At these times she appeared aloof and cool. But when she made the rounds with the psychiatrists and physicians, things changed. She displayed a smile, warm voice, fluttering eyelids, and even touch. The difference in her behavior was obvious and never ceased to amaze her staff.

The other administrative position was held by Venita Hall, the supervisor. The nursing staff had very little contact with her. She usually communicated to the staff through Kelsey. Most of her time was spent either in consultation with Kelsey or sitting behind her desk. The staff was never certain what her responsibilities were except to conduct the yearly evaluation conference.

Kelsey and Hall were good friends who operated in tandem. They would leave the floor together for lunch and coffee breaks. If any of the staff left the floor at the same time, it was always clear that Kelsey and

Hall would sit at a separate table. They never joined the staff even when members of the staff were eating alone.

The nurses, nurse aides, and orderlies did the hands-on work with the patients and functioned mostly independently. The charge nurse for each shift assumed many of the head nurse responsibilities.

THE PROMOTION

The staff found the MHU to be an enjoyable and challenging place to work—as long as they avoided Kelsey and Hall. The rule seemed to be "avoid the top brass and avoid conflict." New employees were cautioned to "go about your business" and to "avoid the top" if they didn't want to get "cut down." That approach seemed to work. Most of the nurses were extremely competent and functioned well on their own. Even those who received special favors would admit that the floor functioned effectively without much leadership from Kelsey and Hall.

Kurbing worked for approximately six months as a staff nurse, rotating all three shifts. She enjoyed her relationship with her peers. They seemed to respect each other and were friendly and cordial during and after work hours. She found her job to be rewarding because it allowed her to demonstrate her ability to perform leadership roles when working as the charge nurse. She was not satisfied with the head nurse and supervisor. They were not effective role models. They weren't fulfilling their responsibilities, which meant that the rest of the staff had to fulfill them without being compensated for it. After a while, Rebecca fell into the same pattern that everyone else did—avoid the top brass and avoid conflict.

One day Kurbing received a memo asking her to meet with the head nurse, supervisor, and director of the hospital. Her first thought was "What have I done now?" But when the meeting began, Kurbing heard the first positive comment from either of her superiors in six months: "We have noticed your leadership style and your ability. We see you working effectively with both the patients and other staff. We feel you have the qualities and abilities we are looking for. Will you be the new head nurse for the MHU?" The supervisor—Hall—was going to become a nurse clinician, and Kelsey—the head nurse—would become the supervisor. Kurbing pondered the motivation for this offer. Was the administration aware of the ineffective leadership? Had they created a new position to remedy the problem, or had the supervisors requested a position change merely to push the work onto someone else? Kurbing gratefully accepted the compliments but requested some time to consider the offer regarding the new position.

Kurbing had many factors to consider before accepting this position. Was this an opportunity to effect change within the unit? There was so much that could be done that wasn't. Was she too young and inexperienced to do it? Would she inherit the negative perceptions that were held for the current head nurse? Or would she have an advantage being a liked and respected member of the "group"? Were the obstacles to an effective work environment insurmountable, or could the position provide new opportunities for change? A week later Kurbing met with the same three individuals and accepted the position. She was to assume the new position in one week.

Kurbing was eager to begin the new position and maintained a positive attitude. But when the staff change was announced, she met with both expected and unexpected responses. Several staff members congratulated her and said they looked forward to the positive changes that would occur. Another said, "One more week and you'll be one of them!" Others expressed pity and sympathy: "You poor thing. How can you ever work with them?" Sister Mary Francis with whom Kurbing had often worked and who had helped orient her to the MHU expressed noticeable displeasure. Kurbing could see her mouth drop as the announcement was made. After the meeting, she approached Kurbing and said, "I can't understand why you got this position. I've been here a lot longer. This hospital is my order. And you're not even Catholic!" Kurbing was shocked but could respect her feelings. She assured her that she had neither sought nor requested the position. In fact, she was quite unsure of accepting it. Then Kurbing said that it was having quality nurses on the staff like Mary Francis that gave her the confidence to give the position a try. Sister Mary Francis's mood changed from anger and jealousy to one of surprise and, hopefully, understanding.

Finally, Kurbing began her first day as head nurse. In the morning, she made the rounds with physicians and became oriented to the new position. When lunch time arrived, Hall and Kelsey approached her. Kelsey said, "Of course, now that you're the head nurse, you will no longer eat with the other members of the staff. You will join us at *our* table." What a surprise! Kurbing had never even thought of being so arrogant. In front of other staff members standing nearby, she replied, "I appreciate your invitation, but I can't function as head nurse unless I keep contact with my staff. And eating lunch together is an important part of that process." She heard snickers in the background as Kelsey said, "OK then, we'll just go without you." Kelsey and Hall looked at each other, pouted, and walked toward the elevator together. No one ever said a word to Kurbing about the incident, but it sent a strong message to the staff. She would not become a pawn in the hands of the supervisors.

TWIN PREFERENCE

As head nurse, Kurbing was responsible for scheduling all employee hours. A long-standing complaint among many of the nurse aides was the fact that twin sisters were given preferential treatment in the work schedule. They had been on the unit staff for over twelve years and preferred to work days only. Others on staff preferred days but were not granted that privilege. They worked both day and evening shifts as specified in the nurse aide job description.

At first Kurbing didn't know how to handle this situation. She could ignore it. She could continue the current practice for a while and gradually make a change. Or she could make the change and post the new hours, surprising everyone. But none of these solutions seemed right.

After a week of contemplation, she scheduled a staff meeting concerning hours requests. At the meeting she explained to the staff her new responsibility of making out all hours and requested their cooperation and patience in making this transition. She reassured them that all specific hours requests would be honored if at all possible and also read the portion from the job description relating to the requirement for all aides to work rotating shifts. She stated she would schedule hours in such a way as to follow this description. She could see the looks of surprise and pleasure on some of their faces. But no one said anything about it during the meeting.

After the meeting, several staff members approached Kurbing individually and expressed pleasure with the new "fair" approach. The twin sisters left the meeting without comment. Everyone knew (and Kurbing knew that they knew) they were the only ones working strictly days. Therefore, Kurbing felt she needed to take the initiative and approach them. Within a half hour after the meeting, she asked to speak to them and in an open and honest manner tried to explain to them what she perceived as being an unfair practice in relation to other staff members. She reassured them that she understood their preference for days and that with the number of college students employed who preferred the evening shift, it would not be often they would need to work an evening, but on occasion it would be necessary out of fairness to others. Although not pleased with the change, they understood. One said, "We wondered how long we'd get by with this."

When the schedule came out for the coming month, the twin sisters each only worked two evenings the whole month. However, Kelsey, the unit supervisor and former head nurse, confronted Kurbing immediately: "Don't you know that Laura and Linda never work evenings? You have them scheduled for several, so you'll just have to change it." Kurbing told her supervisor of the staff meeting they had and also that the hospital's policy was being violated by never rotating them to the evening shift. Kelsey reluctantly agreed that this was true. Kurbing also assured her boss that she had spoken individually with Laura and Linda and that they understood the reason for change.

Several months later when Laura, Linda, and Kurbing were having coffee together, Linda said, "By the way, thanks for giving us those couple of evenings on the hours sheets." Kurbing responded, "I'm confused. You prefer days, so why the thanks?" Linda replied, "The rest of the staff is so different to us. We're both enjoying work a lot more—even the young ones are nice to us now." Kurbing knew she had made the right decision when she initiated the change with the first schedule, and she knew she would get positive feedback from some of the employees, but she was surprised when the twins recognized the value of everyone following policy.

PATIENT CARE CONFERENCES

Kurbing effected other improvements as she worked into her position. She didn't endorse change simply for change sake, but she did value it and initiated it if it improved a situation. As a staff nurse she had always been concerned about the lack of patient care conferences. These conferences are important for providing continuity of care. This is particularly important in a mental health unit where varying approaches are utilized. For example, should they encourage patients to express their feelings, or will they ruminate in self-pity and would distraction thus be best? They also had part-time employees who would benefit from specific instructions about care.

When she suggested twice-weekly care conferences, the staff resisted: "We've never had them before." "We're too busy to take time for a meeting." "That's the job of the nurses, not the aides and orderlies." Kurbing explained her rationale for having care conferences and asked the staff if they would be willing to give it a three month trial period. She guaranteed them that the conferences would take no more than ten minutes. They agreed to try, "but only for the trial period."

The name of the patient discussed at each conference was posted the day before the conference, and one nurse aide was asked to spend extra time with the patient before the conference to provide insights with the group. All staff attended the conference except for the ward secretary and one nurse who remained accessible to patients. The permanent night nurses and orderlies were requested to give input by tape recorder. They provided insight on problems and suggested solutions.

The first few conferences were a challenge. Staff tended to wander off the topic. They needed to be guided back to the patient's care if the conferences were to finish in ten minutes. But this was the first time that many staff members were involved in any significant decision-making process. It wasn't long until staff members themselves kept everyone on track during the brief session.

For the first month she heard excuses. "I'm in the middle of something and can't come." "I don't know the patient very well so I won't have anything to say." But over the three-month trial period, she noticed an increase in attendance and participation by all members of the staff. At the staff meeting to evaluate the care conferences, someone said, "How did we ever run this unit without care conferences?" The nurse aides and orderlies particularly liked them. They had a chance to contribute and felt more important in these meetings.

PROBLEM WITH NANCY

One day during lunch several staff members were chatting. One complimented Kurbing's abilities as head nurse. Another said, "Yeah, if Nancy would just shape up and get with it." Kurbing asked, "Is there a problem with Nancy?" Nancy was an RN who worked as a charge nurse straight evenings (at her request). Kurbing had never really gotten to know her. "Nancy is really mad about you being head nurse," one of the other nurses said. "She thinks she should have been asked because she's worked here longer and is older than you." Another added, "She mouths off about it a lot to the evening shift, but they all know her and know that's the way she is."

Kurbing's impression of Nancy was that she was a somewhat aloof, often cynical, yet competent nurse. Should she confront her? Was this merely gossip? Would the problem go away? She could try to reach out to her at the change-of-shift time, but Nancy might avoid her. Nancy's best friend and roommate worked on the MHU as an RN, too, so Kurbing thought perhaps she could reach Nancy through her roommate.

One day a nurse called in sick for the evening shift. No replacements were readily available, so Kurbing realized this might be an opportunity to communicate with Nancy, who was scheduled to work that evening. "If someone had to work a double shift," Kurbing thought, "why not me? I've done it before."

Nancy came to work and noticed another nurse was ill and absent. She began to ask others who was coming in to cover the evening shift. Kurbing intervened and said, "I'm planning to stay on and work a double shift tonight." Nancy was shocked. "But you're the head nurse!" Kurbing responded, "Yes, and that means it's my responsibility to make sure there is adequate coverage on every shift." Nancy quickly added, "I suppose you'll work my charge position then tonight?" Kurbing assured her, "No, you're the charge nurse. I'm merely taking Carol's place on the shift and will assume her duties and responsibilities." They never discussed Nancy's feelings toward Kurbing. From that night on, however, Kurbing felt a different attitude from Nancy.

Six months after she accepted the position as head nurse, Kurbing was offered another position at a school of nursing and accepted it. She left Metropolitan with mixed feelings. She felt she had accomplished a great deal for the well-being of both patients and staff. She felt awkward about avoiding Kelsey and Hall, but this probably saved a lot of headaches. Overall, it was a time of learning, a time for growth both personally and professionally.

QUESTIONS FOR DISCUSSION

1. How would you describe the communication climate on this floor of Metropolitan Hospital?
2. What leadership styles do Kelsey and Hall have? How does Kurbing's eventual leadership style differ from Kelsey's and Hall's? Is Kurbing an effective leader?
3. Why does Kurbing respond with caution to the promotion offer?
4. What makes it possible for two adults (the twins) to work in an environment in which they sense that they are disliked because they are given preferential treatment?
5. Why was there a change in how the patient care conferences were perceived? What does it say about the previous communication climate that the nurse aides and orderlies "had a chance to contribute and felt more important" after the care conferences were established? What type of decision making does this reflect?
6. Was it appropriate for Kurbing to respond the way she did to the "problem with Nancy"? How else could she have dealt with Nancy?
7. What are the implications of Kurbing's feeling "awkward about avoiding Kelsey and Hall"?
8. Kurbing is in a position to lead a transformation at Metropolitan Hospital. What could be the future for the hospital?

SELECTED BIBLIOGRAPHY

Mintzberg, H. (1995). The manager's job: Folklore and fact. In S. R. Corman, S. P. Banks, C. R. Bantz, & M. E. Mayer (Eds.), *Foundations of organizational communication* (pp. 193–196). White Plains, NY: Longman.

Planty, E., & Machaver, W. (1977). Upward communications: A project in executive development. In R. C. Huseman et al. (Eds.), *Readings in interpersonal and organizational communication.* (pp. 159–178). Boston: Holbrook.

Simon, H. A. (1995). The fine art of issuing orders. In S. R. Corman, S. P. Banks, C. R. Bantz, & M. E. Mayer, (Eds.), *Foundations of organizational communication* (pp. 193–196). White Plains, NY: Longman.

Tracey, W. R. (1981). Putdown techniques: Are you guilty of them? In R. C. Huseman et al. (Eds.), *Readings in business communication: Strategies and skills* (pp. 156–160). Hinsdale, IL: Dryden.

OUTERWEAR, LTD.

Gary L. Peterson

Outerwear, Ltd., is a privately held corporation manufacturing men's and women's outer clothing. Its product lines are prepared under various labels and purchased by major department stores and by catalog distributors for their operations across the United States. Clothing lines produced by Outerwear are generally regarded as upper-end-of-the-line quality.

Business for Outerwear, while cyclical according to seasonal lines, has steadily increased over the past several years. Employment in peak times now numbers well over 250, with only lack of space and lack of qualified, trained power machine operators preventing the company from adding even more help. Monthly output tops $1 million in goods during most production periods.

The organizational structure of Outerwear emphasizes the divisions involved in clothing manufacture. The major functions are design and pattern preparation, cutting, (sewing) operations, shipping, and administrative services. Most employees work in the sewing operations division, where employment fluctuates between 125 and 160 operators.

The typical operator is female, age twenty-four to forty-five, and Asian American (primarily one of the recent refugee cultures of Cambodia, Vietnam, or Laos, with some Korean). Administrative officers and staff, including supervisors, are Caucasian except for two supervisors who are young African American women. Facility with the English language is a problem for many of the Asian American women operators. For several, a translator is necessary for extended conversation or instructions. Operators are paid on a piece-work basis. The operation is a union shop, with workers represented by the Amalgamated Garment Workers. Productivity, speed and accuracy, and quality control are stressed throughout the organization.

Among the key personnel involved in the company are Dan Bryan, vice president, operations; and Mrs. H., operations manager.

The ranking executive of the company on-site, Mr. B. is twenty-nine years old and has been with the company for six years. He is assertive, confident, and willing to accept responsibility. He is chiefly responsible for local operations but is in daily contact with two marketing vice presidents, as well as purchasers and business agents for clients. During his six years at Outerwear he has seen business triple. Mr. B. is regarded by almost everyone at Outerwear as outgoing, personable, friendly, very approachable, decisive, and knowledgeable about the entire range of Outerwear's business.

Mrs. H. brings forty-three years of experience in the garment industry to her position, including seventeen years with Outerwear. Her start in the industry was in New York City. She is generally regarded as being the person who has "trained" Bryan, providing the benefit of her background and experience. Mrs. H. is seen as extremely powerful, as one not to cross, as one who means something when she says it. Confident in her knowledge and experience, she is not inclined to be patient with mistakes or comfortable with a participative management style.

It is early lunch shift at Outerwear, Ltd. Jenny Armour, one of the production supervisors, slumps on the bench and against the wall in the lunchroom as she chats with Irene, who works in Design.

Jenny: I don't know why I stay here. I don't have to put up with the abuse I get for trying to do my job.

Irene: What's happened now? Is the line down?

Jenny: No. We were ready to start on cut order 6327 this morning, right? Just as we were getting under way, Mr. B. comes running in with a change order from the buyer. They want the camel coat with one pocket, not two, and here we are all geared up to go with the two. Hey, I know these things happen, but I hate to get it on such a short notice. Fortunately, we caught it in time to save the final sewing of pockets, but we sure have a big stack of wasted camel pockets all cut out.

Irene: Where was Mrs. H.? How come Dan had to bring the change? Incidentally, I haven't heard about the change yet.

Jenny: That's why I'm so upset! Dan couldn't raise Mrs. H. on the intercom or in her office. He knew we were near pocket setting so he came right to me. But fifteen minutes later, here comes Mrs. H., and when she saw the stack of material for the second pocket there, and nobody working on it, she lit into me like only she can do. She does it with Rhoda, and probably Cass and Arlene, too. Do you know how I feel when that happens? Here I am working with three operators on the cutting mechanism of their new machines, and right in front of them I'm blessed out. I had everything under control, and she didn't even give me credit for that. I finally was able to tell her that Dan brought the change order and wanted it implemented right now, and that he wasn't able to reach her. All she said was, "OK, OK. You have the change made?"—and off she went. Then, wouldn't you know, because of the change we started late, and some of the ladies were doing things wrong. They won't wait for me to get them straight. They ask whoever's been here the longest and off they go. I can't get all twenty-five at once, and they won't wait for me. So, more mistakes; and Mrs. H. was here to see those, of course, and I catch it again. And here it is not even noon yet. Any more coffee in that thing?

The scene shifts to Mr. B.'s office. It is nearly lunchtime, and Dan Bryan is meeting with Ted Parsons, sales representative for Business Computer Systems, to discuss a timetable for deciding on the purchase and installation of new computer systems at Outerwear, Ltd.

Mr. B: [As phone rings] Excuse me, Ted. [to phone] Hello...Larry? Yeah, glad they could find you. What did you discover about that shipment for Carsons in Cincinnati? The coats went out of here last Tuesday.... Yeah, by United Parcel.... Yeah, I've called them here three times, and they assured me everything was on schedule.... OK. Call me when you know for sure. Still going to meet with Doug this weekend?...Good. Go easy with him on that rich food.... OK. Talk to you later. [to Ted Parsons] Now, let's get on with this schedule. I've told you we want to make the changeover while we're down and preparing for spring orders.

Ted: That should be no problem, once we have found out what you need for the software systems.

Mr. B.: [To Renny Wills, design director, who is at the open office door with jacket in hand] What is it, Renny?

Renny: Sorry, Mr. B., but the buttons requested for number 4310 are here, but they aren't the right color.

Mr. B.: Let me see. [Holds button to coat] You're right. That is not what we ordered. Have you talked to Standard Notions?

Renny: No, sir. Not yet. I thought I'd check here first to see if you wanted to go ahead with the buttons they sent us.

Mr. B.: No. They won't do. That is not what the customer ordered. Better call Standard and get the right buttons on the way. Mighty quick. Never mind...I'll call.

Renny: But our schedule says we run the 4310 tomorrow. They are promised for early next week.

Mr. B.: They'll just have to wait. I'll call them and explain. They won't be happy, but neither am I. [to Mr. Parsons] Sorry for the interruptions. [Turns to phone, checks a number on a clipboard, and dials] Helen? ...Dan Bryan here at Outerwear, Ltd. We're all set to run a new order with the buttons you just sent us, and they are not the right color...OK. I'll hold a moment. I think the invoice is number 292416. [to Parsons] See the kind of details we'll have to have on the computer? [to Helen, on the phone] OK. You find it? What's the number?...Right.... No, that is not what you shipped.... No, it's not. What you sent is at least two shades darker than the sample we have here—if we have the correct samples.... Yeah. That must be it.... OK. You have them on hand?... How quick can you get them to us?...We'll return the wrong ones, so don't bill us double, OK? Thanks for your help.

During the phone conversation, Mrs. H. has come to the office door. She steps in, acknowledging a hand wave from Mr. B., and waits for the phone call to end.

Mrs. H.: Dan, did we get a late change on the camel car coats?

Mr. B: Yes, we did.

Mrs. H.: I wish you'd tell me when that happens.

Mr. B.: I did. I wrote it up. It's in your mailbox. Any problems?

Mrs.H.: No. I don't think so. Jenny says she has caught it. She's a capable supervisor and I won't worry about that. What about the extra cuttings?

Mr. B.: See that they get back to Cutting. We have more of that fabric and I think another order is on the schedule. Check that out for us, will you? I'll call you back on it.

Mrs. H.: [As she leaves, speaking mostly to herself] Our luck, it will be bigger pockets they want.

Mr. B.: [Turning once again to Parsons, who is still there] Software systems, eh? That will be Jerry's area. He really should be meeting with us. I'll give him a call.

QUESTIONS FOR DISCUSSION

1. How well is the line organization responsibility working at Outerwear, Ltd.?
2. How would you describe the communication climate between Mrs. H. and her supervisors?
3. What suggestions do you have for the supervisors at Outerwear? Explain and justify.

4. Describe the primary communication behaviors of Dan Bryan, Mrs. H., and the supervisors.
5. This case illustrates differing approaches to how managers view and deal with subordinates. Discuss the implications for these approaches.
6. What recommendations would you make to Outerwear, Ltd., in regard to organizational structure? To Dan Bryan in his role as executive? To Mrs. H. in her role as operations manager? To the company for overall improvements in handling its routine communication linkings and needs?

SELECTED BIBLIOGRAPHY

Brass, D. (1981). Structural relationships, job characteristics and worker satisfaction and performance. *Administrative Science Quarterly, 26,* 331–348.

Browne, C., & Nietzel, B. (1952). Communication, supervision, and morale. *Journal of Applied Psychology, 36,* 86–91.

Conrad, C. (1983). Power, performance and supervisors' choices of strategies of conflict management. *Western Journal of Speech Communication, 47,* 218–228.

Downs, C., & Conrad, C. (1982). Effective subordinacy. *Journal of Business Communication, 19,* 27–37.

Ivanevich, J. (1979). High and low task stimulating jobs. *Academy of Management Journal, 22,* 206–222.

Kelly, L. (1982, May). *A critical review of the literature on superior-subordinate communicative relationships.* Paper presented to the International Communication Association, Boston.

Renwick, P. (1975). Perception and management of superior-subordinate conflict. *Organizational Behavior and Human Performance, 13,* 444–456.

Tjosvold, D. (1984). Effects of leader warmth and directiveness on subordinate performance on a subsequent task. *Journal of Applied Psychology, 69,* 422–427.

SECTION 4

Recognizing Leadership and Management Styles

CASE 10
The Globalization of Technomed

CASE 11
Life Is: Debits, Credits, Tick Marks, and Taxes

THE GLOBALIZATION
OF TECHNOMED

Scott Hammond and Robyn Fearon

PART 1

"Welcome to Technomed," the electronic voice said as the group of executives triggered the automatic door. "Please use the security system at all times if you are an employee. If you are visiting for the first time, please press the red button by the elevator, and a security guard will help you."

The team of managers used their security badges to call the elevator. Behind the cold black glass, they could see the silhouette of the security officer checking to see whether all the team members applied their cards to the magnetic reader. Most workers were used to the high security of Technomed. They came and went under the watchful eye of the "Gestapo." They even learned to open their bags when there was a random check to show that they were not taking any "corporate secrets" home with them. It seemed funny to many that the company was so tight on security. People often joked about the security. Some said it was the military background of a former manager that led to the high security. Others said they were trying to make the company less profitable so they would not have to pay bonuses. But every once in a while a manager would come across a real corporate secret, one that would be incredibly valuable to a competitor. That knowledge kept the complaints about security from getting too loud.

When the team of managers pushed the button to the eighteenth floor, the security camera light went on. They knew the guards were having a second look. They didn't know that the guards were not concerned with security but with gossip. For the last two weeks, there had been a steady stream of senior managers going up to what was referred to as "the president's floor." Teams of managers from all over the company had been summoned in small groups to meet with the developer and chief executive of Technomed. The president's floor was the only place in the building that was not watched with security cameras.

The eighteenth floor was the private domain of Ron Hardcastle, the chief executive of what had been called one of the most innovative and aggressive biomed firms in the world. Hardcastle began his career as a young chemist with a competing firm. As a twenty-two-year-old intern, with only a master's degree, he had proposed a streamlined process for the manufacturing of antibiotics. With confidence and naiveté, he drew up a plan that would cut manufacturing costs by 70 percent. His moment of glory turned sour, as colleagues gave him 101 reasons why it would not work. Some behind his back, and others to his face, said that someone as young as he with only a master's degree could not possibly know what he was doing. Besides, "We're the only ones who make this product, and we'll be just fine."

Hardcastle's sponsor fought to keep him from being "eaten alive," but within two weeks Hardcastle left the company. He borrowed his uncle's garage and began testing his idea. Within a few months he had proved his results. A few months later, he presented his findings to Medical Technology Limited, a small single-product firm that had a license to manufacture generic drugs for overseas sales. Hardcastle did not sell his process to Medical Technologies Limited, but he did land a job as director of manufacturing and a seat on the board of directors. Within six months, on Hardcastle's twenty-third birthday, they changed the name of the company to Technomed.

Through the next ten years, the company grew by leaps and bounds, mostly because of Hardcastle's innovations. Hardcastle first focused on the manufacturing systems and found ways to make higher-quality medicine at a lower cost. This attracted numerous licensing agreements. Later, Technomed began partnering with research laboratories and manufacturing new products. This forced the growth of marketing, sales, and distribution divisions of the business. The systems thinking that Hardcastle had learned as a chemist proved extremely valuable in understanding the business systems of the organization. Within a few years, he was named CEO of the company he had privately thought of as his.

For the next twenty years Hardcastle was the high-profile, personal leader of this company. Because of the nature of the business, the company spread into seventy-nine different countries. Hardcastle proudly said that he had visited every office in the company. Although that was not exactly true, it was pretty close. At first Hardcastle would charter a plane and go on site visits. Eventually the corporate jet was purchased, and the president began making more and more site visits every year. The site visits became important because the company began to have a sense that Hardcastle was connected with them, no matter how remote their assignment was.

During that twenty-year period, Technomed acquired several other companies. This usually worked well, but sometimes the acquisitions were awkward and ill conceived. For example, in 1985 Technomed bought a small research-oriented firm called BMD (British Medical Devices) in the United Kingdom. The firm owned a particularly valuable patent, and Technomed's main reason for purchasing BMD was to take over the patent so they could manufacture and sell the drug. At the same time, Technomed was spending millions of dollars to develop a hair growth product that would compete in the United States with other products on the market and would still meet the requirements of the Federal Drug Administration. Technomed was denied a patent. It was told by the patent office that its product was too similar to the one that it already owned. BMD had already solved this problem. When Hardcastle asked why his firm had not been told about the BMD patent, the Brits who still ran that division said, "You didn't ask."

For Hardcastle this was the first of several incidents that told him that he was no longer in control of "his" company. He would sit for hours and wonder whether the company was too large. Why had innovation dropped off? What happened to the aggressiveness that built the company in the first place? Were they paying too much attention to the stock prices and not enough to the future? Hardcastle had no answers to these questions, but he knew that his people knew how to solve the problems.

Operation Expertise

When the elevator doors opened on the eighteenth floor, the senior managers were greeted by a receptionist who escorted them into a large conference room. It was clear that the room had been prepared for them. They were seated around a large table. All of the instruments of corporate communication were in the shadows around the table—flip charts, overhead projectors, laser pens, and LED projectors, even a video conferencing system that would allow them to contact any Technomed office in the world. After a short wait, Hardcastle entered the room.

"Welcome," said Hardcastle. "Thank you for coming from such far-away places. I know for some of you this is the first time at company headquarters. I want you to know that the guards don't really carry machine guns. (Laughter) Seriously, I appreciate you coming in. I am looking to you to solve a problem which will save this company. To begin with, let me ask you a question. Was your bonus bigger this year? Bill?" Bill was taken by surprise and hesitated. "Come on, Bill, you're with friends. Did you make more or less?"

"Less."

"Less, but not by much. Right?"

"Yeah."

"But what if it keeps going down at that rate? What if you project the decrease out five years, then what do you have? (Silence) If you keep projecting out five years, then you will be paying me a bonus just to keep your jobs. (Muted laughter)

"The truth is that what worked for this company yesterday, what has been making us a whole lot of money in these last years, is not going to be what does it for us in the future. Let me show you some graphs that tell us where we are headed, but they don't tell us why. The first is the most distressing. It represents our overseas sales, which peaked at $132 million in 1990 and have declined almost every year since then. In 1997, we are projected to go below $100 million for the first time since 1980. [Figure 10.1]

"There are two problems with this. First, we all know that the overseas markets are the growth markets. If we had to rely on what we do here in the U.S., well, we would have been auctioned off a couple of decades ago. We have always been at our best in finding unique markets overseas and exploiting them. That's the reason this company exists."

"The second problem is seen in Figure [10.2]. It tells us where the industry is headed. As you can see, the competition is not just in our backyard—they are trying to knock down our bloody door!

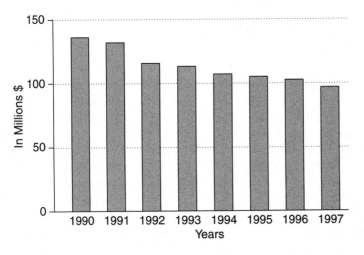

FIGURE 10.1 Technomed Overseas Gross Sales

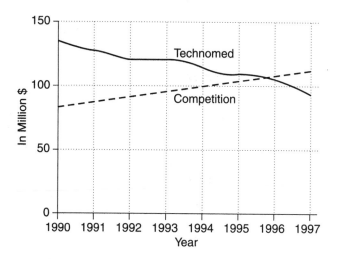

**FIGURE 10.2   Overseas Sales Compared
to Competition**

"As you can see, if we take the average overseas sales of three competitors, we no longer 'own' the territory that we used to. We've been invaded, and I don't like it. My guess is that as bonus checks go down, you won't like it, either. Most of the growth opportunities in our business are coming from the Pacific Rim, specifically China. No offense, Jean-Luc, but the Europeans have their own way of doing things, and we don't often fit in. But we can really make hay in China and other Pacific Rim countries if we really go for it.

"Your assignment as a team, should you decide to accept it (laughter), is to help us find a way out of this mess. For the next few hours, I have a group of the finest consultants and internal experts available who will give you the information you need."

The group sat quietly as a young accountant prepared his presentation. They were stunned at the significance of their assignment and wondered what had caused Hardcastle to pass this along to them. They wondered whether they would be asked for advice, whether this was some kind of setup, or whether they would really have a say in how this problem was solved. The accountant began with a one-hour presentation that detailed what Hardcastle had alluded to in general terms. Domestic and European sales were flat, all other overseas markets were declining, and this was a long-term trend. Other competing organizations had begun to erode the company's distribution network and seemed to do a better job of managing regulations in different markets.

The next two presentations were stunning. The first was presented by a diversity/cultural consultant, a professor from the local business school. It was clear that she did not have an in-depth understanding of the Technomed business, but she had clearly identified some significant concerns. The main question was how these concerns related to the business issues.

The Queen of Culture

"My name is Dr. Lark Lanai. My students affectionately call me the 'queen of culture.' I teach international management in the business school, and I write extensively in cultural anthropology. At the request of Ron Hardcastle, over the last year my graduate students and I have collected data from your organization using internal records, interviews, focus groups, and survey instruments. I have data regarding several problems that I will describe as issues."

Issue I.   "The first issue is a difficult one. In our surveys, we found that fewer people believe they have personal contact with top management, that they are relying more on policies and procedures and less on the advice they get from their bosses. We all know the significance of Ron's leadership over the last years. Well, Ron still gets out, but he has more places to go and less time to get there. The company has grown to the point that Ron no longer has a personal touch in every corner. As a result, you are moving from a personal style of management to an institutional management.

"There are some other related issues. We find more and more that employees in your company don't know the people they work with. When Technomed first came into a country or market, they formed a team and the team stayed together for some time. Recent increases in marketing efforts have meant that you are transferring people more. As one of the people we interviewed said, 'We treat people like interchangeable parts now, not like family.'"

Issue 2.   "This issue is related to the first issue. Despite all the talk about diversity in the last few years, this company is becoming less diverse. Oh, sure, the ethnic numbers are changing here and there, but overall you are attracting people who are less diverse. For example, for a while you had what was called the Princeton Mafia working in one division. (A chuckle came up from the room, but Lark did not crack a smile.) People complained that the only way to get a promotion or a bonus in that division was to have a Princeton MBA. Well, even though accounts of this were exaggerated, it represented the fact that you tended to hire people who think like you, who are educated like you, and who have similar life experiences. As one interviewee said, 'It's not overt; it just happens that way. I hired Bill because I knew him in school and know I can trust him. He hires his associate, we become friends, then we hire others who seem to fit. Before you know it, we have a bunch of clones running the company.'

"Another interviewed employee said, 'When we first went global, we hired just about anyone who knew anything about our business in the local market. Some of them did not work out, but others were great. They taught us things that we never knew about the markets we served, and I would like to think that they learned something from us, too.'

"Consider the chart now displayed [Figure 10.3]. The number of multinationals working in this company has gone down in the last five years, while the number of U.S.-trained MBAs has gone up. That's not to say that MBAs are bad; it's just that the organization needs some intellectual diversity if you are going to be a global company.

"Our team of researchers did some digging and interviewed some of the non-U.S. managers who had left. One Japanese manager said, 'In my country changing companies is like changing families. It is very difficult. But I was working in my position when my boss retired. He was widely respected in headquarters and in Japan. It was expected that one of the three juniors would take his place. But headquarters decided to bring in an Australian. They said it would be for a few years and then there would be another manager. In my culture, I am so very dependent on my boss.

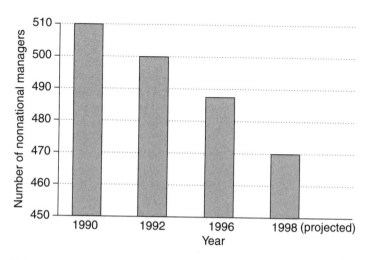

FIGURE 10.3   **Non-U.S. Nationals as Managers**
in Technomed

He is like my father and priest. I cannot abide having him change every three years. So when an opportunity came with a competing company, I took it. Those opportunities are rare in Japan.'

"Another Chinese manager, who helped Technomed develop the Hong Kong market, simply said, 'I found that it would be difficult, if not impossible, to go any higher in the company. If you don't golf and you don't speak MBA, then you don't have a chance to share your ideas in a language they will listen to.'

"Those who are staying are not happy, either. Our general survey of managers shows morale declining overall, but morale among non-U.S. managers is down even further. As we tried to pinpoint the cause of this, we interviewed one U.S. manager who replied, 'When I came out of business school, my specialty was international management. I spoke Chinese and was in the top of my class, and so within a few years, I was a product manager in the Hong Kong office. During that time, my product was successful, but I became increasingly frustrated with my assignment. I found that as long as the system was in place for marketing and distributing the product, I could make some incremental progress. But I found myself fundamentally unequipped for developing new ideas or making new progress with my Chinese peers. I suspect that they were a lot more frustrated with me than I was with them.'"

As Clear as Milk

The third presentation was also done by a consultant. He was one of those touchy-feely kind of people with too much energy and deliberate vagueness. He came from Birdhouse Associates, Inc., a U.S.-based training company that believed everyone and everything should have their life completely planned out thirty minutes after being born.

While the first half of the presentation was a collection of commonsense phrases about time management, leadership, and even personal hygiene, when he turned his presentation over to a young MBA to give data, there were some interesting findings. He told the group of a longevity study within the company of four hundred middle managers. The survey had asked the questions shown in Figure 10.4 over a three-year period.

The Birdhouse consultant's analysis focused most heavily on question 2 and moved too quickly to diagnosis. He seemed to be saying that the senior managers should write a vision and transmit it to the organization and then give really good motivational speeches so that everyone will buy in. Ron Hardcastle cut him off: "Thanks. This has been real helpful."

Hardcastle then excused the experts and turned to the group of managers. "You are a group of high-performing managers from all different parts of this company. Each of you has been selected because of your

FIGURE 10.4   Birdhouse Associates Survey Results

1. The major function of Technomed is to:

Percentage agree:	1994	1995	1996
Make a profit	33	39	45
Help individuals grow	31	25	19
Provide employee security	29	21	12
Other	7	15	24

2. I have a clear sense of the mission of Technomed.

Strongly agree	34	28	22
Agree	44	39	20
Somewhat	11	12	12
Disagree	6	7	12
Strongly disagree	6	14	34

3. I see Technomed as a place with a future.

Strongly agree	24	18	12
Agree	40	36	22
Somewhat	11	10	10
Disagree	16	17	12
Strongly disagree	9	19	44

4. Technomed is a company that values innovation.

Strongly agree	44	38	32
Agree	24	29	18
Somewhat	7	8	9
Disagree	16	17	19
Strongly disagree	9	8	22

5. I am confident that Technomed management understands the global nature of the business.

Strongly agree	24	18	12
Agree	34	29	20
Somewhat	11	12	12
Disagree	6	7	12
Strongly disagree	25	25	44

ability to solve problems creatively. I need you to work as a team and a half and make some sense of this data. Help us figure out what is wrong and especially how we can fix it. At the end of your time together, I need a clear definition of the problem and a good list of 'hows' and 'whats.' You can use this room to meet. I think we have everything you need, and if we don't, we'll get it for you. Right now I'll give you a couple of hours to get your heads into this thing and come up with some questions. Then, I'll be back to see how you are doing."

PART 2

Hardcastle was clearly exasperated when he entered the room. He had spent the first hour away from the group cornered by the consultants who were trying to tell him, on the one hand, how undefined the problem was and, on the other hand, how complicated it was. He blew up when one of the external consultants suggested that the people he had called together had no idea how to solve the problem. When he was cornered by one of the team members who complained about things being ill prepared, he really got frustrated. He began speaking when he entered the room.

"Look, to begin with, I know that you are having a hard time telling where to start. If I could tell you I would. But you need to know that just because the definition of this problem is not very clear does not mean that it is not very important. Your jobs, the future of this company, and the health of the world is at stake. Not much, just that. So if that can't keep your attention, then we don't need you here anyway.

"What we know is that we have to globalize. What we know is that we have been geocentric, sociocentric, and probably egocentric about how we have done it. What we know is that we have to bring the notion back to our work teams that we can and will make better use of their local expertise. We can do that if we adopt a more interactive communication practice. Because of that, we need new metaphors, new models and a map about how to get there.

"This exercise is about how we do that. Rather than having our corporate training folks roll out another program, we want you to tell us how you can work in each of your groups better. Some time tomorrow, I would like each of you to present the how of this to me. Tell us what and why and when and how and anything else that might help. You might start first with a definition of the problem. Tell us what you are trying to fix; tell us why it needs fixing, and then tell us how to fix it. Now is that so hard? (Laughter) Now I'll take questions. Yes?"

"What kind of resources do we have to work with? I mean, some things we might think up cost money, and that's been hard."

"Don't worry about money. If the reasons are there, then the resources will be. I would rather spend money on a low-cost, high-impact solution that on a low-impact, high-cost solution. But I will spend money to solve this problem."

"What is the scope of our focus? Do you want us to look company-wide?"

"I think it is a company-wide problem, but I am not sure that the solutions are company-wide. Some of them are very local. I would hate for us to come up with some sort of one-size-fits-all solution and not take into account that things are different in New York than they are in Lima. Tell me how we can make your work teams better before you tell me how to improve the company."

"What kind of format do you want for our presentations?"

"I'm easy. I don't need formal unless you want formal. But I do need clear. Please be clear about the problem, the reason for the problem, and the plans you propose. I'll see you tomorrow."

Sally Reed, the vice president for Human Resources, stepped in after Hardcastle left the room and said, "There will be a number of international visitors here tomorrow to see your presentations. I hope that they are creative and communicate across cultures. We wouldn't want our message to be washed out by our means." She turned and walked out of the room.

QUESTIONS FOR DISCUSSION

1. How did Hardcastle frame the problem? What assumptions are made? Do you accept those assumptions? Why or why not?
2. What are the cultural issues involved in the framing of the problem? Do you accept those issues?
3. What are the communication issues involved in framing the problem?
4. What are the various cultural issues that each group must navigate to gain support for its proposal?
5. What are the communication issues that each group must navigate to gain support for its proposal?
6. Can you find examples of any of the following attitudes that could pose difficulties for the teams in problem definition and resolution: geocentrism; sociocentrism; gendercentrism; ethnocentrism; egocentrism?

SELECTED BIBLIOGRAPHY

Cummings, T. G., & Worley, C. G. (1997). *Organization development and change* (16th ed.). Cincinnati, OH: Southwestern College Publishing (especially Chap. 21, "Organization Development in Global Settings").

Elashmawi, F., & Harris, P. R. (1993). *Multicultural management: New skills for global success.* Houston, TX: Gulf.

Gudykunst, W. B., Matsumoto, Y., Ting-Toomey, S., Nishida, T., Kim, K., & Heyman, S. (1996). The influence of cultural individualism-collectivism, self construals, and individual values on communication styles across cultures. *Human Communication Research, 22,* 510–543.

Jackson, S. E. (Ed.). 1992. *Diversity in the workplace.* New York: Guilford.

Schwartz, S. (1994).Are there universals in the structure and content of values? *Journal of Social Issues, 50*(4), 19–45.

Weiss, A. (1998, July). Global doesn't mean "foreign" anymore. *Training Magazine,* p. 55.

CASE **11**

LIFE IS: DEBITS, CREDITS, TICK MARKS, AND TAXES

Tim Singleton, Martha H. Merritt, and David E. Morris, Sr.

George Thomas leaned back in his chair, propped his feet up on his desk, and decided to take a break after a very busy morning. His mind wandered to the complex and perplexing issues that he faced as staff supervisor when an obviously upset Sue Torres stormed into the room. Torres angrily told Thomas that she was certain that Mr. Smith had been listening in on her phone conversations again. "George, I do not have to put up with all the nonsense that goes on around here. I can always find another job, even if it means leaving public accounting," said Torres. Without even waiting for a response, she turned and left his office. Thomas had been wrestling with this and other problems for several months and knew that if things did not improve, the firm would probably face losing some good employees, including Torres. Over the next few days, Thomas took time out to reflect back on the structure of the company, his responsibilities as supervisor, and existing and potential staff problems.

Thomas had joined Smith, Jones, & Co., CPAs, seven years ago as a staff accountant at a time when the firm was growing rapidly. He had served as professional staff supervisor and audit partner of the firm for two years. In this position, he had the responsibility for supervising all staff accountants in the firm, as well as responsibility for all work done in audit or review engagements; and as partner, he had, along with the other partners, unlimited liability for all work produced by the firm.

Smith, Jones, & Co., CPAs, was a small firm that operated as a general partnership, with three partners. Jim Smith, Jr., as managing partner, had the overall responsibility for managing the operation of the firm, making the final decisions with regard to hiring/firing, reviewing other partners' work, soliciting new clients, and maintaining good relations with all clients. The third partner was Ron Wilson. He had joined the firm as tax partner when Jim Smith, Jr., became managing partner upon his father's death. Wilson served as the tax and management advisory services partner and had responsibility for all work done in tax and consulting engagements. The firm also had seven staff accountants with varying degrees of experience who reported to Thomas. There were two secretaries, one reporting directly to Mr. Smith and the other to both Thomas and Wilson (see the organizational chart for the firm in Figure 11.1).

The firm was founded by Jim's father, Jim Smith, Sr., in 1948. The elder Mr. Smith died of a heart attack while working late one night at the office during tax season. He was working well in excess of seventy hours per week during that time of year and, apparently, the stress was more than he could tolerate, even at forty-two years of age. Jim, Jr., who was twenty-two years old at the time, was serving as his only other partner. The elder Mr. Smith's last words to his son were said to have been, "Jimmy, if something happens to me, make sure those tax returns are mailed on time." The younger Mr. Smith was proud to be carrying on the family business and believed firmly in his father's business practices and continued to live by them. Smith was also proud that, like his father

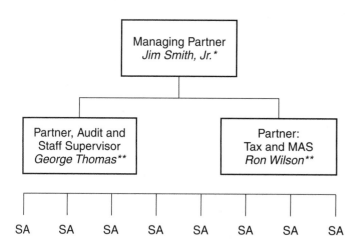

**FIGURE 11.1   Organizational Chart
Professional Staff
Smith, Jones, & Co., CPAs**

*Secretary A reports to Smith

**Secretary B reports to Thomas and Wilson.

before him, he was a model citizen and community leader. A lay leader in his church, Smith always sat with his family as close to the front of the church as possible. After church, he would quickly go to the back of the church to greet others as they were leaving. He would also give to various charities and made sure that he was chosen to serve on the board of directors or as honorary chairman of such organizations. He often talked to others about his importance in the community.

George Thomas, too, was a family man with a beautiful wife, Joan, and three beautiful children, Will, David, and Michelle. Thomas enjoyed his free time doing such things with his family as hiking in the mountains, fishing, and attending his children's school activities. He also served as a lay leader in his church and enjoyed all of his church activities. Thomas felt very fortunate to have a wonderful family and a good job. Unlike Smith, who seemed to do things based on how they would help his standing in the community, Thomas did things because he enjoyed them. He also understood that employees often have obligations to their families as well as their jobs—another concept that seemed impossible for Smith to grasp.

Thomas attempted to project staff assignments on a quarterly basis. To accomplish staffing successfully, he requested a weekly update from each of the other partners regarding upcoming engagements (i.e., new engagements, additions to/deletions from existing engagements, and staffing needs). He then combined engagement needs and available staff into an assignments matrix. The quarterly assignments matrix could then change weekly based on partner updates. The quarterly matrix was submitted to the partners weekly. The staff accountants received an updated assignments matrix on a weekly basis as well, but it covered only the next four-week period.

When staff accountants requested vacation, they had to do so at least three months in advance and were not guaranteed the time off until four weeks before their vacation period began. All professional employees were allowed vacation based on length of service with the firm. Employees with less than one year of service had no vacation; from one year to two years, one week of vacation was awarded; from three to ten years, two weeks of vacation were awarded, but the weeks could not be taken consecutively. After ten years, three weeks of vacation were awarded, but, again, the weeks could not be taken consecutively. Changes in firm engagements and employee vacation requests, along with sometimes incomplete information on their needs from the other two partners, made staffing a real challenge (see an example of a four-week assignments matrix in Figure 11.2).

Recently, Thomas had heard from several staff accountants who were unhappy with the vacation policy, as well as with certain other

FIGURE 11.2   Staff Assignment Matrix

		Smith, Jones, & Co., CPAs			
		June 5–30, 19XX			
Assigned	Number	June 5–9	June 12–16	June 19–23	June 26–30
Staff	1	Tax Plan A & B	Audit C	Audit C	Vacation
Staff	2	Audit L	Aud L/Tax Plan N	Tax Plan P, Q	Tax Plan R, S
Staff	3	Audit M	Audit M	MAS O	MAS O
Staff	4	Audit H	Tax Plan G	Audit F	Audit F
Staff	5	Audit H	Tax Plan I, J, K	Audit F	Audit F
Staff	6	MAS D	MAS D	Vacation	Tax Plan E
Staff	7	MAS D	MAS D	MAS D	Vacation

Note 1: Clients represented by letters A, B, C, etc.

Note 2: MAS = Management Advisory Services

policies. Many of these policies had apparently been in place since the inception of the firm in 1948. However, there were no written office policies. If there was ever a question about policies, the question was addressed to Smith. Thomas thought that Smith believed that the office policies that had worked since 1948 need not be changed. He also believed that Smith would not be very open to changes in policies that might, in any way, decrease the workload of the employees or the profits earned by the firm. All professional staff members worked on strict time budgets and were required to have a specified minimum number of billable hours per week. Smith always instructed Thomas to make sure the time budgets were tight on all assignments because he believed this would motivate employees to work harder to meet their standards. He also told Thomas, "Motivated employees are happy employees and thus are more productive." However, if the standards were not met (i.e., the jobs not completed in the time allowed), employees were required to complete the task on their own time. Smith was also heard quoting his late father, "I remember when I was young, people were lucky to have a job at all and would never think of complaining about the pay or the work schedule. I felt fortunate when I did not have to work sixty hours in one week." Therefore, Thomas had not discussed any of the current concerns of the staff with Smith.

One of the staff accountants who appeared unhappy was Tim Walton, a bright young man who had been working for the firm since graduating with an accounting degree nine months previously. Thomas had been very pleased with Walton's professional growth at the firm. Walton was married and had two children. He had recently expressed dissatisfaction with the firm's policy regarding overtime. Overtime, when required, was scheduled from 7:00 P.M. to 9:00 P.M. Regular work hours ended at 5:00 P.M., allowing two hours for dinner before returning for the scheduled overtime. Walton had stated that this arrangement sometimes caused him to be as late as 11:00 P.M. getting home. He said that he would much prefer to work straight through until the work was finished, allowing him to have more time with his wife and small children. Thomas knew that Walton placed a great deal of importance on spending time with his family. When Walton was initially hired, he told Thomas, "I am very pleased to be working here. You seem like a person who understands the importance of a family to a young person like myself." Thomas had heard similar complaints regarding overtime from others on his staff.

Walton had also been distressed by a recent discussion with Smith. Walton had suggested that the firm might wish to think about advertising. He had noticed advertising by other CPA firms in the area and thought it might help the firm to attract new clients. Smith's response was that of anger: "Are you crazy? Advertising is for used car dealers and convenience stores! If you think the firm is on that level, you should be looking for another job." Walton did not understand Smith's response to his suggestions and was hurt and upset by his remarks.

Another problem that staff members, including Walton and Sue Torres, had difficulty dealing with was the firm's handling of phone calls. The policy discouraged personal calls, which certainly seemed reasonable to Thomas. However, staff members complained that the policy was being enforced by monitoring of their phone calls. Although Thomas was not personally aware of any such monitoring, he had heard the rumor for a long time that Smith and his secretary listened in on private conversations. Staff members considered this an invasion of privacy, as well as an indication of a lack of trust by the firm.

Related to this problem was the fact that Smith read E-mail addressed to the employees. The staff had a strong basis for suspicions since Smith would mention things to employees that he otherwise could not have known. Thomas knew for a fact that Smith did read E-mail. Smith told him that it was his right to do so since it was his computer equipment. He indicated he had discussed the issue with his attorney who said, in his opinion, that it was probably legal.

Torres had joined the firm fourteen months ago and was currently dating an employee of a company that was a client of the firm. Thomas knew this but did not think it created a conflict of interest since the boy-friend did not have any financial duties. However, after apparently learning of the relationship, Smith gave the entire firm, including Thomas, a long lecture on the improprieties of firm members dating clients' employees. Torres and Thomas believed this lecture was aimed directly at her. Torres became upset because she felt Smith should have discussed this issue privately with her and also because she felt, frankly, that it was none of his business. Once again, she told Thomas how unhappy this situation made her and that she would give up her job, if necessary, instead of ending her relationship with the gentleman.

Another office policy disturbing some staff members was the company requirement that they be CPAs or working toward that goal while, at the same time, the company refused to reimburse staff members for the cost of taking continuing professional education courses required to maintain a CPA license. Staff members believed the firm should reimburse them for course fees, meals, and lodging, as did most accounting firms.

Finally, Smith had a policy of conducting staff evaluations only on an annual basis. Thomas believed the staff needed evaluations more frequently to help them with professional development. However, Thomas was afraid that Smith would see an increase in staff evaluations as wasted time and effort.

After giving these problems a great deal of thought, Thomas finally did ask Smith whether, as staff supervisor, he might be allowed to implement changes in office policy. He did not specify which policies, nor did Smith ask him. Smith responded that he could do so but to keep in mind that any decrease in quality or quantity of staff output would not be tolerated. Furthermore, he told Thomas to remember that no one was indispensable. Thomas took this comment to include himself, as well as his staff. He left the meeting unsure how to proceed.

QUESTIONS FOR DISCUSSION

1. What conflicting interests does Thomas have as professional staff supervisor? If you were Thomas, how would you resolve the issues? Should he use participative management in setting standards? How could the staff contribute positively to this standard-setting process for firm operations? What are some of the risks of staff involvement?

2. The monitoring of E-mail by employers is a fairly common practice and is apparently legal. However, several court cases are still pending. Do you think it is ethical for employers to engage in such activity? How would you feel if you were asked by your employer to read staff E-mail? If you felt it was unethical, would you still do it, or would you refuse? What might the consequences be of either choice? What do you think are the effects and implications of such a practice at Smith, Jones, & Co.?

3. Performance evaluations are important for both managers and subordinates. Employees need to know "where they stand." How often should employees be evaluated? Should evaluations be very formal or informal? Should they be in writing or oral? How are performance evaluations critical to the success of the firm, as well as to the career advancement of the individuals working within the firm?

SELECTED BIBLIOGRAPHY

Articles discussing the issue of E-mail privacy include the following:

Bjerklie, D. (1993, April). E-mail: The boss is watching. *Technology Review,* pp. 14–15.

Cappel, J. J. (1993, December). Closing the e-mail privacy gap. *Journal of Systems Management,* pp. 6–11.

Kallman, E. (1993, December). Electronic monitoring of employees: Issues and guidelines. *Journal of Systems Management,* pp. 17–21.

Kingston, J. S. (1993, October) How private is employee use of e-mail? *Communications News,* pp. 22–23.

McMorris, F. A. (1995, February 28). Is office voice mail private? Don't bet on it. *Wall Street Journal,* p. B1.

Building Group and Team Effectiveness

CASE 12

A BEARING JOINT VENTURE

Roger D. Vincent

"We have the acquisition," Jack Laughlin told Roy Desota, "and I want you to go to Hanover to see how their human resource policies will mesh with ours at the Albion plant." Laughlin had been working on a joint venture with a German firm for well over two years, and finally, they had given the go to continue.

Laughlin Industries manufactures bearings for differentials in the automotive industry, and the Germans had developed a special technique with roller bearings that had a different metallurgical property to them. This in turn created less friction in the bearings, wherever used, and therefore created a huge reduction in the amount of torque required to run engines and all drive train parts. All this combined to save auto manufacturers money and would increase Laughlin's market share, *if* they could work with the German company in a joint venture arrangement. It would all depend on the plant in Albion, Michigan, where the new process was to be installed and operated by the German company, Kauff Bearings.

BACKGROUND

Laughlin Industries was a privately owned, closely held company with corporate headquarters in Kokomo, Indiana. It owned seven manufacturing facilities and had just completed construction of a new research and development center in Vincennes. Jack Laughlin was the CEO and chairman of the board. His father, Harry, had retired and turned over the control of the business to Jack. Harry had controlled the company very tightly and was well known in the industry as one who could seize the opportunity to make money when others couldn't. He had been very successful, but most of the organizational culture under Harry had been very traditional. His son represented the new generation and believed it was time for the company to realize it was no longer just a small company doing well in spite of itself.

Desota had just been hired in July by the Laughlin company as the new corporate director of management planning and development. As such, it was his responsibility to help the management at Laughlin develop its skills to take on the additional responsibilities required as a result of Laughlin's success and growth strategies. Having extensive experience with high-involvement, participative management culture, Desota was convinced that the Laughlin Corporation was in desperate need of such a culture, and Jack Laughlin agreed.

Horst Hanneman, the Kauff plant manager, had insisted the add-on operation at Albion be independent of the Laughlin operation. In other words, Kauff Bearings would be a plant within the Albion plant. Hanneman never openly said so, but his actions plainly revealed his misgivings and lack of confidence in the Laughlin management side of the Albion plant.

In October, Roy Desota traveled to Hanover to assess the management approach used by the Germans and to see whether it was in alignment with the culture he envisioned for the Albion joint venture with Kauff. When he returned from Europe, he was convinced the Germans were eager to try the version of the management culture he described, and they saw very little conflict with the components he had presented and the management strategies they intended to employ on the Kauff side of the facility.

BUILDING TEAMS: A NEW CULTURE

By the time Desota arrived at Albion, the new team leaders for the Kauff side had been identified from the ranks of Laughlin workers, and the production manager, Orrin Henderson, had come from an older Laughlin plant in Battle Ground, Michigan. Henderson, like Harry Laughlin, his longtime boss, was from the old school of managerial thought. In his view, managers were to command and control. The new human resource manager, Merideth Langston, was hired from outside Laughlin and was eager to try out and learn how to implement many of the components of the new culture Desota had described to her.

Langston and Desota set out to design the culture, quickly gaining support from Hanneman. They developed a pay-for-skills system and an organizational structure using autonomous work teams as the key component. The organization's structure would permit people to work in self-managing teams, giving individual team members greater interaction with their coworkers and greater responsibility and authority for a broader scope of work. Each team would be responsible for a broad spectrum of work including not just operating the equipment but taking ownership for planning, safety, and personnel issues and developing a keen sense of business acumen. The approach emphasized cross-training, learning new skills, and increasing each team member's skills in the total team task. Since the team was considered the basic unit for performing work, the team leader role would be very critical. The team leader was primarily responsible for bringing the team to a level of self management. Furthermore, an extensive employee selection system using behavioral assessment centers, as well as peer performance appraisals, would be implemented. When these components were in place, Laughlin began the process of hiring employees.

The team leaders had not been involved in the development of these components, and neither had Henderson because they were in Germany learning the technical side of the business. When the team leaders returned, Desota and Langston set about bringing the team leaders up to speed on the culture and their role in it. Henderson, unfortunately, didn't see things that way. He saw team leaders as "his men" who were to carry out his directions. In addition, he disagreed with their title as team leaders, wanting them to be called supervisors. Desota relied on his organizational pull to convince Henderson to keep the team leader title, and he told himself that he would eventually have to deal with Henderson.

THE MOMENT OF TRUTH

The first team of new hires arrived on a bright summer day in June. The Laughlin management team had planned extensively for the intense two week training program demanded by the new operations approach. As a group, the new employees were bright, eager to learn, and excited about having the opportunity to work in a new culture in which they would be treated as business partners and adults who would make many business decisions. They practiced endlessly: role-playing conflict resolution, giving and receiving criticism to one another, and working on effective team meetings. This was an excellent team, and at the end of two weeks Desota believed he could have asked them to take down a telephone pole and they would have completed the task without tools!

On Henderson's return from Germany, there was a first-day-on-the-job meeting with the brand-new team, all the staff, the engineers, Hanneman, Langston, and of course, Henderson. Everyone was excited;

there were smiles, an attitude of can do—it was almost utopian. Then, Henderson took the microphone. Frowning, he looked at the team with cold, penetrating eyes and said, "I don't know what kind of horse crap you people have been given over the last two weeks, but let me tell you how it is. First, these are the rules of working here. They are not flexible and neither am I." Instantly, the team smiles all vanished. All eyes fixed on Desota. There was a look of betrayal on their faces. Desota looked down at the floor, realizing it had taken exactly fifteen seconds to undo all the planning and work of the previous six months.

QUESTIONS FOR DISCUSSION

1. Was the Laughlin culture suited to the Kauff Bearings culture? What would you have done to ensure a better fit?
2. Was there an inherent problem with having a "plant within a plant"?
3. What could/should have been done with the production manager to have prevented the conflicting philosophies?
4. Where do you think Kauff Bearings went from here?
5. As Roy Desota, what would you do—in this public meeting with all team personnel present? Afterward?

SELECTED BIBLIOGRAPHY

Patten, T. (1981). *Organizational development through team building.* New York: Wiley.

Cohen, S. (1993, June). *Designing effective self-managing work teams.* Paper presented at the Theory Symposium on Self-Managed Work Teams, Denton, TX.

Woodman, R., & Sherwood, J. (1980). The role of team development in organizational effectiveness: A critical review. *Psychological Bulletin, 88,* 166–186.

Browning, L. (1977). Diagnosing teams in organizational settings. *Group and Organization Studies, 2,* 187–197.

Dumaine, B. (1990, May 7). Who needs a boss? *Fortune,* pp. 52–60.

STAR WARS, INC.

Scott Hammond

It just was not working. A year and a half into the Tiger project and the software group was six months behind. The group building the casing was three months behind. Operations vice president Gregory Hart was angry. From his office in Sunshine, California, he could look out the window and see the buildings that housed the two divisions. Hart had come from the software division, where, it was said, he was responsible for building the team culture. This success had launched him into senior management of Hightech Weapons Division.

On this day, however, Hart wished he were back at his workbench with "a good technical problem to solve." The casing and the software groups were behind; and the hardware division, building the most critical and complicated part of the advanced weapons system, was on the phone asking about test dates. Not only did he assume that the hardware group was going to ask for an extension, but he wondered why they had one of their staff scientists calling and not the project leader.

Hart had seen many late projects delivered to the federal government, but these days that particular client was much more demanding and much less flexible. When Hart and Star Wars, Inc., first got into this business, Star Wars was the only company bidding for the government contract. Now a half-dozen businesses were serious contenders. "The government knows that and is just plain more demanding of us," Hart was fond of saying. "The Tiger project was a chance to put our company on top again. In some ways it was a custom-fit project for our company. I believe the government chose our bid because we had a division that could do each of the critical components. Our software group, our casings group, and the hardware group together could do it all," he further speculated. He reminded himself that the hardware division took the design and was building a beta model. The casings group was building the

117

package, and the software group was interfacing the control systems. Only a few of the components were subcontracted out. It's a real sweet deal for us. If we build a working beta model, then it's almost a sure thing that we will get the contract to manufacture the Tiger."

Hart continued musing, "We have a lot of confidence in our three groups, but the hardware group is really the unknown for us. They are in a remote location in the Midwest. They were acquired three years ago from another company, and this is the first time that we have worked with them on an integrated contract. In addition, they are not used to the pressure of government contract work. Also, in the Tiger project theirs is by far the most complicated element. The casing should be simple, an adaptation of previously used designs. The software is a little more complex but not something that has not been done before. But the hardware design is unique. It is really pushing the leading edge and applying technology that has never been used. We spent a lot of time convincing the client that our group could do it, but I have my concerns. They are basically a bunch of scientists and engineers who do most of their work on computers. This is a chance for them to really build something."

Hart took the call from the hardware division staff scientist. "Mr. Hart, I really didn't need to talk to you. I just wanted to know what the schedule is for testing the beta unit. We've heard that some of the other groups are behind, and we want to know if we are sticking with the current schedule."

Hart knew that if he changed the current schedule, he would have to notify the client, but he also knew that the other groups would not be ready for the test. He was waiting to find out how bad things were at the hardware group before talking to the client. So, expecting the worst, he replied to the question, "I don't want to put you in a bad position, but I am concerned about your group being on schedule. Software is six months behind...."

"Oh, no," said the hardware division scientist. "That won't do; we'll be ready for the beta testing in six weeks."

Hart hung up the phone and asked himself, and then others, why the group with the most complicated element of this complicated project was two months ahead of schedule while the groups with the less complicated parts of the project were behind. After a phone call to the project director for the hardware component, Hart confirmed that their group was indeed ahead. He decided to make a visit to the site to find out why things were going so well. Within three days Hart stepped off the plane in a medium-sized midwestern city to visit the hardware division.

What Hart found was surprising. He reminded himself, "I was part of the team effort in the software group. In fact, I was one of the chief sponsors of the team program. I thought we did a pretty good job at sponsoring a collaborative culture until I met the people in hardware."

Hart was met by Bob Baker, the division leader, and by Dan Turner and Sandra Howard, the team leaders. He was surprised that they were casually dressed, even though they were meeting someone from the corporate office. He also noted that they were on a first-name basis with most of the people in the plant. One technician stopped the group in the hall and asked Baker if he would be playing basketball with them at noon. "Not today, Jim. Greg's here from corporate."

After a tour of the plant and an impressive presentation by the Tiger project leaders, Hart sat down in the plant conference room with Baker, Turner, and Howard. The twelve-foot by twelve-foot room off the plant floor was called the Tiger Project Team Room. It contained an overused coffeepot on a table in one corner, a set of folding chairs and a table, and an old refrigerator where the employees could keep their lunches. One wall was almost entirely covered with photos of team members during a project test or at a company softball game. On the other wall was a bulletin board, which held notices of professional conferences and the obligatory safety and Equal Employment Opportunity (EEO) documents. In the center of the bulletin board was a notice for the team Christmas party, which was at least three months old.

Hart was surprised during the meeting how various team members came in and poured themselves a cup of coffee even when the "big wigs" were having a meeting. "How did this all get started?" Hart asked. Baker explained that four years ago, while the hardware division was still a part of another company, they reorganized the company into a "team organization."

"At that time our division was really struggling," said Baker. "We were supposed to be a scientific research organization, and all we had were a bunch of individuals going out for small-time government contracts. What we needed was a central focus. We needed to start competing for the bigger projects that are more profitable, with fewer competitors. Meanwhile, our parent company put us on the chopping block. They could see our problems, and their solution was to sell us. After they indicated that they were trying to sell us, they stopped paying as much attention to us. This allowed me to sneak out from under the corporate policies they imposed and try something new."

Baker continued, "All our people said we should try the team approach. When it came to teams, we really didn't know what we were doing at the time. I thought that we would have a few company rallies, put up some posters, and hire some consultants to teach everyone how to hold hands. But once the concept got going, we quickly found that it was much more."

Howard added, "We started with a restructuring. There were several scientists and engineers in management positions who were very frustrated. We created positions where they could move back to their technical work without a reduction in pay or status. We called them "Technical Leaders" and assigned a few young scientists to work with them. Then we eliminated the middle manager position in favor of the team leader position. Now team leaders are assigned based on projects."

Bob Baker cut in. "It's like in football having a team captain for one game and then assigning another for the next game. Our senior scientists are asked to be team leaders for the duration of the project based on their particular expertise. When the project is over and another one comes along, they might just be team players for that one."

Howard said, "That way our managers are not exposed to the threat of technical obsolescence, which can kill your career in this business."

Baker added, "We also began to adjust the salary scale so that we could bring all the scientists in line based more on their technical contributions. We could see that many of our customers were coming, not to visit with management but to visit with staff members or groups of scientists and engineers. So we decided that if our customers were recognizing our staff members' contributions, then we should as well."

What puzzled Hart was how they got such a program going. In the software group they had done some restructuring but mostly focused on trying to change individual attitudes about teams. So, he confided to the team leaders, "At the software division we spent most of our effort on training the staff members about teamwork. They spent time with a consultant working on team development. Some of the teams even went on retreats together, where we did ropes courses and river runs. Overall, morale was pretty high."

"We did some of that around here," said Baker. "And we are still doing some of it. But we found that we couldn't just focus on one thing. We needed to take a broad perspective and look at the salary system, the culture, and the people."

"Initially we didn't have the money to send everyone out to 'charm schools,'" Howard added. "So Bob told us that whatever we did to build our team had to focus on a work-related problem. That turned out to be the right thing to do for the wrong reason. We have since found that some of the team-building exercises are quite good, but only if there is a work-related focus. I think our morale is better than it was four years ago, but not because we feel better about each other. It's better because we work better. We still have just as many conflicts as we did four years ago, but in this new culture we have ways of dealing with them."

"How did you do that?" Hart wanted to know.

So Howard told him: "We began by having an external consultant sit in on our team meetings. She would help us establish the ground rules and then periodically would interrupt the meeting to talk about the process we were using. She would focus on functional and dysfunctional behaviors and suggest ways of dealing with our problems. After a while we got tired of paying a consultant every time we wanted to have a meeting, and we found that we could do this ourselves. We designated someone in each meeting to follow the team process. That person did not take part in of the content of the meeting but, rather, made sure that we followed the right team process."

"Where do you use training?" Hart inquired.

Baker answered that one: "We insist that all team members have certain skills and a basic understanding of the system we are trying to build. Everyone needs to see the big picture."

"Do you have a training program based on the project technology?" asked Hart.

Baker replied, "No, we didn't think it was cost-effective to develop a training program for fewer than a hundred people; and besides, we didn't want this to be seen as the training department's responsibility. We ask each of our team leaders to work with his or her people to make sure they understand. The team leaders can bring as many people to the team leader meetings as they feel necessary. Those are great places to learn what the others are doing. One team leader assigned his newest staff member to take notes at the team leader meetings for six months until he could get up to speed on the problem. The last thing we want is for our new people to come away with a great understanding of just one piece of the project. They have to see the big picture, too. They have to see how things fit together."

Baker continued, "We have had some problems. Several months ago one of the technicians suggested that he was being discriminated against based on his race. It was a gutsy thing to say there right to the face of his team members. After a shouting match, the team leader and several of the workers came to me and asked what we should do. I took it to the management committee, who suggested that we start a division-wide program on diversity."

Howard added, "We found that many of our workers don't know how to work with people of a different race or gender. They don't know how to deal with matters of race and gender when they come up. In a close team environment this sensitivity is absolutely critical. We decided to treat that incident like a division-wide problem and do something about it."

One issue had been bothering Hart from the beginning of this discussion. His experience as a manager told him how hard it was to change culture, to change the values and the beliefs of those you work with. Yet in this case, the team seemed to be doing it. "Your diversity program is really a cultural change program, isn't it? How have you gone about changing to a team culture and now trying to change to a diverse culture?"

"That's a tough one," said Howard. "In a town like this, everyone is pretty much the same. We all come from the same roots, mostly from an individualist farming background. The culture of the town seems to be the culture of the plant. We have made some changes, but it is always hard. We have begun by being very clear on where we want to go. We make a clear statement of our values, but that is certainly not enough. Education is the next step. In our team-building effort, it was the education that caused so many of our people to come up with ways to make the values stick. They were often the ones who suggested changes in the way we work. The same thing has happened with our diversity effort."

She continued, "For example, our diversity education has led the human resources department to really look at our hiring practices. They see that while we are well within EEO and affirmative action compliance laws, we are missing out on some very good people because we are so homogeneous. They have suggested a change in the recruiting policies and practices that will eventually lead to a more diverse workplace."

"So you are saying that cultural change begins with training?" Hart responded.

"We call it education. We don't want to just train new behaviors or new skills; we want our people to be educated about the values, the philosophical issues related to collaboration, diversity, ethics, the environment, and a number of areas where the skills are not enough. Cultural change begins with education, but not from the training department. It is the team leader's responsibility to either do the teaching or see that the learning occurs and follow it up," Baker explained.

After hearing about the team approach of this division for over an hour, Hart changed the focus of the discussion to the Tiger project. He wanted to hear from Howard, the team leader, about the problems or concerns they might be having. "Things seem to be going well with the Tiger project?"

"Well enough at our end," Howard said. "We are ahead of schedule but are very concerned with the word that the software group is not up to speed. Frankly, as we have interacted with them on technical issues, we have not always been pleased."

"How so?" Hart felt defensive. This was his old group, and he considered them the ideal division.

She replied, "They don't seem to share information within their group well. That makes it difficult for us because we get one piece of data from one person and then a conflicting report from someone else. It is clear their people are writing the code but don't always know how it will all go together."

Baker piped in. "Another problem we have had with the software folks is with management. One of our staffers got a call from their management several weeks ago and he chewed our staffer up one side and down the other for contacting a programmer directly. He said that any time we needed to talk to someone in that group, we should go through him. We're getting to the point in the project where we have to talk to programming almost every day. But we can't get that manager to return our phone calls."

After making some excuses and promising to deal with some of their concerns, Hart said his good-byes and headed off for the second leg of his journey, to visit his old software division.

At this point Hart was concerned that his old group was not as effective as he had thought. His visit to the software division confirmed his worries. The software group had a leading-edge quality assurance program in place. The human resources and line management predicted that defects would go down considerably and productivity would rise. Five years ago they had initiated a team program. To kick off the new program, the management team had gone on a three-day retreat, which involved team-building exercises, such as ropes courses and a day-long river run. The management team all agreed they felt much better about working with each other after the retreat.

Because of their enthusiasm, the group was seen as one of the corporate leaders in team building. Their president reported, "Ours is a team organization," in a recent issue of the corporate newsletter. "Every time we get a chance, we talk teams. Every quarter or so we have a team consultant come in and work with key groups. We have a poster campaign about teams, and we recognize the most effective teams in our monthly newsletter."

Hart spent the day with the software management. He heard reports on the team program and an update on the Tiger project. By their reports, everything was fine with the organization; the problems with the Tiger project were the result of an unreasonable time schedule. After returning to his office, Hart picked up his phone and called several of his engineering friends who worked at the software division. These guys always told it to him straight when he was the boss over there, and Hart suggested that they give it to him straight now.

Bill Harris, one of those engineers, was the first person Hart called. Harris had been with the software division for more than fifteen years, longer than any of the programmers in the company. His technical ability was widely recognized within the company. Customers, other software engineers, and even people from other divisions would seek out his advice when they had a particularly sticky technical problem. When Hart was director of the software division, he had made Harris a supervisor. Now Hart joked, "That was the worst mistake of my management career." Harris added, "Greg, I'm just not a manager, and I don't want to be a manager.

I prefer technical issues to people issues. With a computer, you always know what you're going to get. With people, you never know." Despite Harris's technical orientation, Hart knew he could count on him to give a true picture of what was really going on at the software division.

"Between you and me, Greg, things around here are worse than they have ever been," Harris confided. "Management is really pushing this quality stuff. Two or three years ago it was team building. It's like 'the flavor of the month.' Most of the technical people see these programs as really getting in the way of how we work. It's not that we have anything against teams. In fact, if things really worked the way they suggest, this would be a very good organization. But what happens is that management seems more concerned about how things look rather than how they work."

Hart wanted specifics. "For example?"

"For example, on the Tiger project we spent six weeks dividing into teams and doing team building before we ever really got down to work. Then when it came time to start programming, everyone used the same old approach we used before. We took the code to the manager, who took the code to the project group leader, who took the code to the project leader. There was none of this team stuff—just the good old military chain of command."

Harris continued to complain about management. He suggested that many of the key technical people were dissatisfied because they were "trapped behind a bureaucracy." He said that managers seemed to be focused on the short term and did not have a perspective beyond the next deadline. "Do they understand how long it takes to get software engineers up to speed in this business? It takes two or three projects, maybe five years, before they have enough technical experience to really work on their own. We can't afford to have our people move across town and work for the competition just because our managers want to line their own pockets."

Hart agreed. He remembered seeing the parking places reserved for management at the software building. He remembered too that Harris had pointed out, "Customers come to our company not because of our managers, but because of our technical people." Hart also had to agree that the new bonus program, which was designed to reward technical contribution, was being used to reward managers. The payroll department confirmed that almost 70 percent of the bonus money went to managers, who represented only 15 percent of the population of the organization.

Hart could see that his loyal friend Harris was growing cynical. He no longer trusted management. He was disillusioned with the organization, even though he still found the technical problems challenging. Harris admitted to his old boss, "I used to think this was a great company. Now I think it's a lousy company with great projects. I've stayed here this long because where else can you find projects like this one to work on?"

Hart hung up the phone and wondered what his next steps should be. The hardware group was clearly outperforming the software and casing groups. All three needed to be on the same schedule. It might be easier to slow the hardware group down and let the others catch up, but how could he ever justify doing that?

QUESTIONS FOR DISCUSSION

1. What communication issues contributed to the success of the hardware group? What leadership issues?
2. What communication issues are keeping the other two groups from performing on schedule? What leadership issues?
3. What steps should Hart take to remedy the situation?
4. What is the likelihood of solving the problem?
5. What should Hart do to try to bring the groups together on the same schedule?

SELECTED BIBLIOGRAPHY

Job, A. M. (1987, October 4). GM to use Toyota's production methods. *Detroit News*, Section A, p. 1.

Kerr, N., & Bruun, S. (1983). The dispensability of member effort and group motivation losses: Free-rider effects. *Journal of Personality and Social Psychology, 44*, 78–94.

Ross, R. S. (1989). *Small groups in organizational settings*. Upper Saddle River, NJ: Prentice Hall (see especially Chapter 8).

Zverina, J. A. (1987, December 17). Teamwork puts applicants ahead at Mazda. *Detroit Free Press*, Section C, p. 8.

QC COMES TO COUNTY ROAD SHOP 5*

Regina Locklear

Carolyn Semple, newest county employee in Marshall County and the first full-time quality circle facilitator, eagerly headed for her first briefing with Roy Masero, personnel director, who was also her immediate supervisor. She already had some general background from the job description, from her homework on the position, and from the interview process. Thus, she thought she knew generally what she was headed into, but this early meeting was designed to provide a much clearer picture of what had already been done and where the county was headed with its Quality Work Life (QWL) effort across the sprawling county.

Masero greeted Semple warmly and introduced Eugenia Gilmore from Parks and Recreation as a member of the Quality Circle Steering Committee. "I invited Genia in because she is going to be able to answer more questions than I can, I fear. I can provide background, some county philosophy and goals, but Genia will know better what is really happening in the circles we have in operation at this time. Let's start, though, with your questions."

Semple had enough questions for two days' worth of meetings but led off with what was foremost in her mind: "Mr. Masero, what is the county's primary purpose in moving to the QWL program, including the circles?"

"It's Roy now, Carolyn. OK? I guess the best way to express the county's position is to say we believe in having our employees achieve success in solving their own problems. Their ownership in what they do

*All proper names, including that of the author, have been changed to protect individual identities.

on a day-to-day basis is important. Employees at most levels in this county have always been told what the problems were, how to do their work, and then simply, to 'do it.' When the new county executive was sworn in, he told us all that there were better ways to manage, and that we'd better get used to change. He suggested we review a number of options, and our research led us to initiate the quality circles."

"Several pilot programs have been underway, although all of them are not still in operation," Gilmore added. "One of the first circles was in my department at Parks, but the supervisor there did not want it and, strangely enough, it never did work. Supervisors in those pilot work groups have received quality circle leader training, and others are slated to go through the three-day program soon."

"So where do you want me to start?" asked Semple.

Gilmore replied, "We want you to attend all the training programs that are underway, to observe and get acquainted, and then gradually to work in the circles and take over for the part-time facilitator, who has already returned to his position in the Sheriff's Office. At one of our early Steering Committee meetings, we can review with you in some detail the steps and schedule for adding more circles to the program. I believe you have copies of all those relevant materials. You will not have much of a training role immediately, but eventually you will be overseeing all circles as well as training circle leaders and members."

"Have the employee unions been involved directly in the circle program?" Semple asked.

"Very much so," spoke up the personnel director. "From the very beginning of the planning and implementation of the pilot programs, the unions have had input and have given strong support. The quality circles program really has been in their interest."

Semple had reviewed reports from the Steering Committee but still was unsure where she was going to be spending her time, so she asked, "Where are the circles held? What locations do they use?"

"Right where we think they should be for greatest impact," responded Gilmore. "All circle sessions are held at the primary work site of the group. We have discovered it is critical to hold those working periods at their times, on their turf, and on their terms." Then she smiled widely as she followed with, "That is why you are going to have so much fun adapting to everyone else's schedule, starting with the first assignment tomorrow morning at Road Shop 5, in the north end of the county. Their summer work schedule is on a ten-hour, four-day week, so the one hour circle session meets at 6:00 A.M., the first hour of their work day. I have already set up a meeting later this morning with Arnie Toolson, who heads the Public Works Department, and he will brief you on the other sites in Public Works as well."

After the briefing with Masero and Gilmore, Semple spent a short period going over reports again before she walked down the hall to the office marked Director of Public Works. She knew Arnie Toolson had a big job, one of the largest jurisdictions in the county to manage, but she found him very informed about the work of circles in his department and particularly excited about the success at Road Shop 5.

"Carolyn," he began, "I think it would be valuable for you to know some of the history of Marshall County as an employer, and some background of the place and the people you will visit tomorrow morning. District 5 is pretty much like the other districts in our operations, at least where they have been. You will see lots of changes when you go to the meeting tomorrow, but I want you to know what it was like."

Toolson continued, "Most of our employees in the county have been with us for years. Traditionally, there has been little turnover. Pay and benefits are good, employment has always been assured, and the work is rarely hazardous or ugly. Many of the workers at Road Shop 5 received their positions through the time-honored patronage system. That system is now gone, and as a result a good many of the veterans have had a low regard for their personal value. They have not felt that they deserved their jobs.

"The culture of the Road Shop crew is hard-hat. Although they have recently hired several females, they are mostly a macho bunch of men. You will be entering the world of pickup trucks with gun racks. Although not all of the crew have completed high school, they are far from dumb, as you will discover. In the past, some of these guys felt that they could not or would not sit in the same room together. That's how expressive and explosive they were about their feelings toward others. Now these guys, and an occasional woman, are the grunt workers. They drive the trucks; they haul the asphalt and operate the hot oil machines; they run the heavy equipment on the highways and on the sides of the highways; they cut the brush and weeds; they move the oil, the gravel, the toxic sprays.

"In the new era, with the changes since the last election, all hiring and all performance appraisals are handled on a merit basis. The new exec restructured nearly everything. There used to be forty of us reporting to the county executive. Now there are ten. He also reduced the number and use of county cars, trucks, and other equipment. You will undoubtedly hear about that routinely.

"Maybe I can best describe how loosely the operations used to be by relating a couple of stories that by now have become almost legend in the county. The first concerns a new supervisor on his first day at one of the road shops. The guys were waiting for assignments, and he simply told them he didn't really know anything yet, that they should just do what they did yesterday. One of the crew members had been out sick the day before, so he simply went back home, to do what he did yesterday. The second story the exec tells himself. He made an early practice to get around to all the work sites in all the departments, meeting employees and talking about his goals and about change. At one of the road shops— I won't tell you which one, although I know—he decided to get a soda from the cooler in the break room. He entered his fifty cents and out popped a can of beer. You won't find beer in the cooler anymore, I assure you."

Semple interrupted the director with a question that now had a bit more urgency, as she wondered what her reception was going to be like. "How are they doing with the circle as an opportunity to deal with their own issues?"

Toolson replied, "I can tell you how they did deal with issues, then I will answer your question directly. This was a group with little or no communication with management, and often not much with one another. They were used to dealing with problems by getting mad, stomping off, even fighting on occasion. They were not sophisticated at all about getting what they wanted. They were direct, all right, but impatient, not game players. They were extremely wary of being manipulated into doing what management wanted. I guess you could say they didn't problem-solve as a group. They simply did what had to be done, or what they were told to do.

"So, where are they now? District 5 was one of our earliest pilot circles. They had a good supervisor, and we felt we could see great potential. They began by agreeing that they needed to do something about the handling of tools and equipment. They had no system, no individual or group responsibility. They pinned down the problem, looked at possible ways to solve it, and set up their system. They had to come to us to make a presentation and to have it accepted. We were happy to see the progress; and because it had little or no cost, we approved it and they implemented it. It was a little success, but a major step."

Semple felt she had to ask, "How do they feel about their supervisor? You said he was an effective supervisor already?"

Toolson smiled and answered, "Receptive and effective. The crew likes Phil Hood. You will, too. He is one of their own. He started working for the county, summers only, when he was seventeen, and worked his way up the ranks. The history of Road Shop 5, however, is that they have always been distrustful of anyone above their immediate boss. We are desperately in need of turning that around. That is where you come in!"

So early, very early, the next morning Semple, who knew quality circles and knew enough about being a facilitator that she did not run from this "opportunity," walked into "hard-hat country." She was gratified that Roy Masero was there in his capacity as personnel director to introduce her, but she really had to wonder what the eleven men and one woman assembled in the break room were thinking. She was extremely conscious of the fact that she was replacing the former QC facilitator, a detective sergeant on loan from the Sheriff's Department, who always attended these meetings on duty (gun included). Semple reflected on that image as she was waiting to be introduced, acutely aware of how different she looked in her dark skirt, blue blazer, heels, and white blouse with a dark scarf bow tie.

The meeting room for Road Shop 5's circle was, by best description, utilitarian. Walls were mostly bare, tables long and well used for lunches and coffee breaks, chairs (benches) of the picnic table variety. Semple was self-conscious as she was being introduced, very aware of the uneasy and, she suspected, unusual quiet. The introduction, however, went smoothly, handled informally by the personnel director, and Semple settled in to do what she had told them she intended to do initially: observe and learn.

What she observed was a group readying themselves to move to a new problem. She quickly applied her system of associating names and faces and soon knew the identities of her first circle group members. Phil Hood, the district supervisor, was the circle leader, at least for this session. There were three truck drivers: Gordon, Paul, and Dennis. There were three laborers as well: Ted, Rick, and Vonda, the only woman in the group. Junior and Soony, she determined, were heavy equipment operators: Junior; the grader, and Soony, the backhoe (whatever that was). Bert was a toxic chemical sprayer; Cliff, the dispatcher; LaTona, a sweeper operator.

The first quarter hour of this session consisted mainly of venting frustrations, or so it seemed to Semple. She wondered to herself whether they were ever going to get past the complaining. She was sure she clocked a full fifteen minutes of comments like the following:

- "We wouldn't have any of this crap if Tony G. would pull his weight at administration."
- "The damn county is so cheap they won't even drive out here to look at our situation."
- "If this happened at Shop 3, and they complained, you can bet they'd get attention now."
- "When it really gets dangerous for us, they don't give a damn about our safety."
- "We have to bust ourselves to get their precious roads cleared, but they don't care about us or our safety."

To his credit, Phil Hood allowed venting to go on only so long and then he simply said, "OK. We are agreed there are lots of problem people as well as problem situations. There are a lot of causes, too. What we need to do now is identify what we can, create some lists, and move to what we need specifically." As Semple observed the rest of the meeting, she began to feel better, a lot better, about the possibilities in this group. They were serious about identifying a serious problem, and it was obvious that Hood had some skills at leading them through the processes they needed at this point.

When Semple attended the next weekly 6:00 A.M. meeting, she asked the group to tell her where they were in the process of problem identification and solving. Members of the group seemed uncomfortable as they answered, but their responses made Semple feel better about them quickly. In the next few meetings, Semple gradually moved closer to what she felt was her role. She listened, she observed, occasionally she offered ideas or suggestions, she reflected on how circle members were handling the process, then she began asking for suggestions, reactions, and help. Soon the group members were responding easily to Semple's inquiries and comments. She noticed an appreciable difference, too, when she started to spend time riding with Hood and discovered more about the actual work of the members of the circle.

Over the next weeks and months, the circle at Road Shop 5 continued to make excellent progress with the current problem. At the same time Semple felt completely accepted. Circle members told her that she was a part of their work life now; she also began to feel that she was one of them. She was proud of their ability to work together effectively, if not always smoothly.

As Semple prepared for the next meeting, which was to be a review of the circle's management presentation the following week, she reflected on the internal struggles that had threatened the group's progress. The difficulties with Cliff had been the toughest to handle. Like all the others in the group, Cliff was a volunteer member but had actually lobbied to be included. He was already disliked by most of the other members; and when he was finally in the circle, other group members believed that he would get on the radio and blab to management or to people at the other shops about all that was going on. They wanted Cliff out, and several members had gone to Carolyn to complain. When Semple finally faced Cliff privately, she had simply told him that his membership in the quality circle was in jeopardy and that he had to "work it out" with the group before they could feel he was trustworthy. Cliff told her he would do whatever he had to in order to stay in the circle, but he also wanted her to make the decision and announce it to the group. "Cliff, I can't do that," she had told him. "This group has developed its own norms for some time now, not something imposed from on high, and if you can abide by those norms the circle will accept you. If not, you are out." It was a time-consuming process for the circle, but eventually Cliff was included and had some valuable insights and skills to share.

At the break room the next morning, following a particularly playful opening interlude, Semple relied on the stock-in-trade phrase that had served her so well: "All right. Let's go to work. Our presentation is scheduled for next week, and it is important to remember that what they are going to be looking for consists of four items: First, what is the problem? Second, what is the recommended solution? Third, what does it cost? Fourth, what will management get in return for its dollars? So let's review the problem."

The problem, which had thoroughly involved the circle, while not new, had surfaced again during the past winter season when the county had unusually heavy demands for snow removal. When a snowplow/ sanding truck was in operation, the auger at the rear of the truck, which pulled the sand into it and then spread the sand behind on the plowed area, would plug up. In wet, or especially in cold and wet weather, frozen chunks of sand would not break up, and they quickly clogged the path into the auger. In addition, because the sand for winter was piled up during the summer and fall months, and was not covered or fenced off, children would play in it, often leaving sticks, big rocks, or other debris behind, covered up by sliding sand. Consequently, during the worst of the storm or snow removal periods, drivers would frequently have to stop, get out on hills, on slippery and wet surfaces, in sliding or blocked traffic, and unplug the auger. In short, an already miserable job was becoming even more dirty and hazardous.

Bert, who was leading the circle on this morning review, asked, "Is that clear enough for the big bosses? Good. Now what do we want? What is our recommendation?" The response, from several directions, described a storage system, which members of this circle had designed. Their solution called for a storage area that would be covered and secure, a place where trucks could back in for fill and still have a covering or screen during the fill operation.

Bert continued, "And how did we get to this point? What was the research and findings?" Again, nearly all contributed: "We put all those related problems on the flip chart sheets, plastered all around the room. Remember, Phil, you finally had to yell, 'Stop! Stop!' We also voted, narrowed, combined, talked about, debated, and developed priorities. Then we really went to work. Some of us tested auger sizes and shapes, others tested kinds of sand and sand/salt mixes, others researched costs of construction, others put the data in charts, and those are ready. Ted made those humongous diagrams of the storage facility and how it would work. We're glad you quit your job at Lockheed, Ted, and came back here after college, to work with us. And we have those beautiful charts listing all the advantages to the county, both short-term and long-term."

At this point, Semple became the facilitator/cheerleader. "Are we ready to get management here for the presentation? Does everyone have his assignment ready? Remember, part of our motto is that we all work the problem; we all work the presentation. The responses were animated: "Yeah, yeah. Bring 'em on." "Hey, let's invite representatives from the other road districts, too. Cliff, you be sure to remind them every day on the radio. This one will knock their socks off."

The following week the circle made its presentation to the director of public works, the manager of road maintenance, and a public works engineer, as well as visitors from the QC Steering Committee and three persons from the other road districts. Immediately after the presentation, Semple called the group to attention. "Well, guys, they're gone. It's over. How do you feel?" The reactions were nearly deafening.

Vonda: Absolutely great!

Gordon: This was the biggest project they've approved yet. For them to accept this for inclusion in the new budget year will cost them some bucks.

Junior: You know, this was my first project in quality circles, and you know how suspicious and doubtful I've been. I can't believe this has happened. We've never been heard before. Can I go through the training course now?

Dennis: I love it! Those guys from Number 3 think our circles are just a coffee klatch, that we just wanted to get out of work. They said they had no idea how much extra time it must have taken us because we were really interested. Now they're hyped to do it, but a little scared.

Hood: [Privately to Semple] These guys have never had much self-esteem before. With the practice in problem solving, and some other skills developed, they actually look forward to these presentations. It is exciting for them, isn't it? They look ready to take on the world.

Semple decided that morning that she hadn't been prouder of a bunch of people, ever—unless it was three weeks earlier, when she threw a birthday party for Phil Hood, at 6:00 A.M. no less, complete with cake and ice cream, party hats, and balloons. Maybe that was a better day, the day some of the guys told her to let them know if she ever needed anybody "taken care of." Maybe that was better, "the day the hard-hats became coneheads."

QUESTIONS FOR DISCUSSION

1. What conditions are necessary for quality circles to be successful in reaching the goals for which they were designed? Were those conditions present in the Marshall County Road Shop team?

2. What conditions existed in the makeup and culture of the Public Works employees that might suggest the quality circle approach would have negligible impact or success?
3. What were the positive outcomes of Road Shop 5's apparent successes with quality circles?
4. What suggestions do you have for the next steps for the Road Shop circle? For Marshall County to take advantage of positive outcomes for one circle?

SELECTED BIBLIOGRAPHY

Brockner, J., & Hess, T. (1986). Self-esteem and task performance in quality circles. *Academy of Management Journal, 29,* 617–623.

Dumas, R. A. (1983, April). The shaky foundations of quality circles. *Training, 20,* 32–34.

Franecki, D. J., Catalanello, R. F., & Behrens, C. K. (1984, July–August). Employee committees: What effect are they having? *Personnel,* pp. 67–73.

Lawler, E. E., & Mohrman, S. A. (1985). Quality circles after the fad. *Harvard Business Review, 63,* 65–71.

Marks, M. L. (1986). The question of quality circles. *Psychology Today, 20,* 36–44.

Sims, H. P., Jr., & Dean, J. W., Jr. (1985, January). Beyond quality circles: Self-managing teams. *Personnel, 62,* 25–32.

Stohl, C. (1987). Bridging the parallel organization: A study of quality circle effectiveness. *Communication Yearbook, 10,* 416–430.

TOWNSHIP GOSSIP

Michael F. Welsh

CULTURAL NOTE*

This case study took place during a tumultuous time in South Africa. The long struggle to end apartheid had succeeded, and majority rule had just been established with the election of Nelson Mandela as president. However, the educational system was in crisis. Many forces had combined to undermine any culture of learning in South African schools. These forces included almost forty years of separate—and unequal—education under apartheid; nearly a decade of educational disruption as schools and school children became caught up and actually took a leading role in the political struggle against apartheid; and a political climate during the early 1990s that was highly charged, fractious, uncertain, and even violent.

Dissatisfaction was fueled with the imposition of "Bantu Education," in 1953. This was a system of education openly designed as inferior and discriminatory to supply schooling for black students. The results of the system were its own indictment: (1) more than 50 percent of the matriculants each year failed; (2) passing rates in math and science were between 10 and 20 percent; (3) less than 1 percent of the pupils starting school graduated twelve years later; and (4) for those who did graduate and make it to the university, 80 percent failed in their first year at historically black colleges, the direct result of poor school preparation.

The human costs of this inhumane system were incalculable. The frustration and anger on the part of those caught up in it was seen and felt in virtually every black community and every black school, even at the primary level.

*Note prepared by Judy Wyatt and Ron Atkinson at the University of South Carolina.

During this time, black school leaders found themselves in a particularly problematic and ambiguous position. They were employed by, and thus in some sense representative of, an official system that had no credibility, with themselves as well as with the teachers, students, and parents in their communities.

Within this general context of structural and emotional paradox, black school leaders faced several problems. First, they typically became school leaders without the benefit of formal management training. Second, in times of crisis they were caught between the demands of the authoritarian and bureaucratic education system and the demands of their students, teachers, and communities. Third, management and leadership in black schools was made difficult by a school environment characterized by resource scarcity, rigid rule-bound bureaucracies, and a broader political context in which government education departments, students, parents, teachers, and community groups often had deeply conflicting views about what a principal should be or do.

THE SITUATION

"Township gossip" was what Vera Moloi thought as she listened to a small group of teachers state their case against her. Now in her midfifties, Moloi had served fifteen years as principal of Boitshoko Girls' High School in Pietersburg. She was a strong and capable woman who had worked her way through the ranks as a teacher, head of department (HOD), and deputy principal, and she possessed the qualifications and experience to move to even higher positions of leadership in education. She firmly believed in staff development as the way to build a productive school, and Boitshoko was certainly productive. The school routinely captured top awards with its programs in music and sport. Most important, however, its matric results were always among the very best. As a matter of fact, last year's results showed a 100 percent pass rate.

That had been an event worth celebrating, and Moloi wanted to share the credit with the staff. In early February of the following year, a party was held in celebration and thanks for the best matric results ever. The whole staff was there. Moloi unhappily noticed, however, that a small group of teachers stood off to the side and didn't participate with the other teachers in making the occasion festive. It was that day that she realized the group in the corner were all members of the South African Democratic Teachers Union, or SADTU, as it was commonly known.

Eleven of the forty-one staff members at Boitshoko were SADTU members. It was a strong group of "hard-hearted females," as she recalled, who were experienced teachers in their mid-thirties and early forties. They were not readers or scholars, but three of them did have university degrees; one had a master's degree and was working on a second honors degree. The group had formed at the school in the early 1990s, while Moloi was away on study leave. When she returned, they had asked her to join them. They admired the strength she showed as a principal and wanted her on their side. She declined. Like many teachers her age, she was a member of the National Association of Professional Teachers of South Africa (NAPTOSA) and maintained a loyalty to that group. Besides, she held to an old-time sense of professionalism and was not inclined to involve herself in the kind of political activity in which the SADTU was occasionally engaged, and she certainly would not be seen in the streets doing the "toyi toyi." She suspected that most of her current troubles could be traced to her refusal to join the SADTU.

She thought about all the trivial things she seemed to be wasting her time with this year and how the SADTU members always seemed to be there nibbling at her like ducks.

The year following their celebration of achievements had been somewhat disappointing to her, as that was the first year in her tenure as principal that the matric pass rates had gone down. She knew that the SADTU members had been responsible to some degree, because some had taught the seniors, and yet they absented themselves for SADTU meetings when she and the inspectors sat to evaluate the matric results and point out areas for improvement.

By the end of that year, there was a clear rift between the SADTU members and others on the staff. SADTU teachers met almost every day and always sat together at lunch. They seemed to hold back when it came to discipline, which caused uneven enforcement throughout the school. The other teachers became jittery and felt threatened by the action, or lack of action, taken by this small close-knit group operating in its midst.

During the last parents' meeting of the year, the SADTU members proposed that a PTSA (Parent-Teacher-Student Association) be formed at the school. The parents and Moloi agreed to the proposal, and in February of the ensuing year, the SADTU made all arrangements for an organizational meeting of the new PTSA to which they invited members of the Pietersburg Education Crisis Committee (PECC). At the same time, the Student Representative Council (SRC) was elected without the knowledge of Moloi or the majority of the teachers. Only the SADTU members knew of the election, and they kept it to themselves.

The first parents' meeting of the new year was scheduled for 19 February. As usual with the first meeting of the school year, a large number of parents turned out along with the staff. Not so usual were the other organizations that showed up: members of the PECC, COSAS, SRC, and the SADTU executive were also present.

Moloi opened the meeting with a prayer and welcomed all those in attendance. As was her custom, she reported on the performance of the school during the past year. She noted that she was troubled by the decline in the passing rate and was concerned about some of the pupils and teachers who had been caught up in the era of defiance campaign. She then introduced a member of the Education Crisis Committee who was to conduct the elections for the newly formed PTSA. He solicited nominations for parent representatives, conducted the balloting, and finally introduced the newly elected representatives of the PTSA. He told the parents that the PTSA was going to solve the problems that Moloi had mentioned earlier. He pledged to take an active role in the school and acknowledged parents' hopes that passing results would improve and the school's good reputation would be maintained.

During March, SADTU teachers asked to meet with Moloi, saying several issues needed to be addressed. Moloi called a staff meeting for Friday. The meeting went well, and discussion centered on the code of conduct for the COSAS, which emphasized student and teacher discipline. During this month, Moloi noticed that some of the PTSA parents were frequenting the school but never checked in at the principal's office, as was school policy. When she asked about these visits, she was told that the parents were merely checking on the situation at the school and she need not be bothered.

The next staff meeting dealt with routine information from the circuit office regarding disciplinary problems such as tardiness, absenteeism, and lack of commitment by both teachers and pupils. Moloi also discussed the Science Partnership Project of the University of the North. The discussion was uncomfortably one-sided. SADTU members showed no interest and remained silent throughout the meeting. The decisions reached were later completely ignored by the SADTU group. After the meeting, the SADTU warned Moloi against calling meetings on Wednesdays or Fridays as these were the days set aside for SADTU general and committee meetings. Moloi took note and promised to do her best to keep those days free of scheduled school meetings.

At the end of April, teacher representatives to the PTSA asked to meet with Moloi in her office. She agreed and hosted a meeting that included not only the PTSA teachers but also the deputy principal, the HOD, and the SADTU Site Committee chair. Quite a number of issues were raised, including favoritism, absenteeism and tardiness, and irregularities in organizing trips. The teachers accused Moloi of allowing some teachers to attend university classes during school hours and doing nothing about the problems caused by teachers and pupils who habitually came late or skipped school. Moloi was amazed to hear these things and pointed out that the very teachers making the accusations were the same ones who were never at assembly and did not really know how she dealt with late-comers. She also explained her role and policies in organizing trips

Actually, the group's primary concern was about how she had handled a recent trip by students to the Rand Show. In that instance, she had asked one of the teachers to organize the trip on short notice. Moloi was away from school at that time, so the teacher wrote a letter to parents informing them of the trip and announced the trip to the pupils in assembly. Only the underclassmen were told because the seniors were not keen to go. SADTU teachers thought that they were deliberately excluded from knowing about the trip for some reason, and on the day of the trip they stationed themselves at the door of the bus counting the students as they boarded. In the end, the trip had been successful, and Moloi thought no more of it.

The discussions in that meeting went on for quite a long time until finally Moloi told the group that their accusations were unfounded and that she thought this time was being wasted. She reminded them that she had called several staff meetings in which these very issues had been discussed but that solutions agreed to during those meetings were not adhered to by SADTU members. So, she ended the discussion, but not before the teachers agreed that the duty list and playground duty assignments be taken to a meeting of the general staff so that guidelines could be set for all pupils and teachers on matters of discipline.

The general staff meeting had been called for the next Thursday at breaktime. The meeting went off as scheduled, but SADTU members stood and walked out after about thirty minutes, saying they had to attend a mass meeting. It was 12:10 P.M., and their absence meant that some children were going to be left without teachers after the break. The meeting continued with remaining staff members deciding on the dates for submission for June evaluation questions and the date for starting exams.

The following week, Moloi was scheduled to be away from school serving on the selection committee for the university's Science Partnership Project. On Monday, everything came to a halt at the school as the eleven SADTU teachers staged a sit-in. Moloi was called and returned the next day, Tuesday. When she arrived, she found visitors from a host of organizations already there. It seemed everyone was represented: the PECC, Civic Association, COSAS, SRC, the SADTU executive, SADTU representatives from neighboring schools, and the PTSA. She learned that a meeting had been scheduled for 9:00 A.M., and that she and the staff were invited.

At first, she did not want to attend. She knew nothing of the meeting or its agenda and did not care to be surprised like this. She thought that if there were a problem at the school, the staff and the PTSA should deal with it before outside organizations were brought in. However, some parents and the chair of PTSA convinced her that she should attend. So, reluctantly, she went.

To her immense surprise, the meeting was chaired by a twenty-year-old COSAS member whose agenda consisted of a series of accusations against Moloi. Each accusation was introduced in turn by SADTU teachers. The first was an accusation of corruption in the assignment of promotion posts. SADTU teachers claimed that only Moloi's favorites, and never SADTU members, occupied promotion posts. The advertisements of openings did not reach SADTU members. To this Moloi could only say that the advertisements were circulated to all staff members to read and sign. She said she could produce clear evidence if anyone wanted to see it. She further stated that all applicants were interviewed and the post offered to the most qualified.

Then, she was accused of misappropriating funds. The accuser, another SADTU teacher, said that Moloi had received funds from churches who used the school building as a venue for church services and from collect-a-can (recycling) projects, trips, and school fees. No one knew what she did with the money. Again explaining herself, Moloi said that all moneys received had been receipted and that she would be happy to prepare a full financial report for review by parents and staff. She indicated that she did not want to hire a professional auditor because school funds were limited. "As a matter of fact," she explained, "funds are short because some parents have withheld paying school fees in response to calls from the old Defiance Campaign not to do so." The collect-a-can projects? "Well," she said, "I haven't taken the cans to the recycling depot yet, so no money has been received."

A third accusation involved favoritism. SADTU teachers claimed that other teachers were allowed to register VISTA as full-time students. Moloi replied that the number of courses a teacher registered for were that teacher's business. "What I am concerned with," she continued, "is whether the pupils are taught and that the teacher does not dodge school to attend personal classes. Besides, I'm not aware that there is any such teacher who is doing that." She admitted, however, that there were teachers who were said to be irregular at school. Anyone who must be absent, however, was required to report to her and to complete leave forms. These forms were then sent to the circuit office. "I must say that SADTU members rarely report their absences and never sign leave forms. I consider that unfair."

One SADTU teacher brought up the case of a teacher who was on sick leave for two months before being advised by doctors to go on early pension since it did not appear that she would be able to resume her duties as a teacher. Moloi had announced this news to the staff. Then, when the woman was released from the hospital, she told Moloi that she wanted to try again. She was allowed to come back. The SADTU teachers felt Moloi was dishonest and inhumane regarding the case. The teacher was ill and needed to be at home.

With a touch of impatience in her voice, Moloi responded, "The teacher in question was not convinced she had to leave teaching because of her illness. A principal cannot and should not just drive a teacher away. Another fact of this matter is that the doctors had not made any official statement regarding her condition. As soon as that teacher is satisfied that she cannot go on, then I will take it from there!"

Still a fourth SADTU stood up to make another accusation. This time Moloi was charged with keeping school property at her home. Items such as a TV, a computer, and garden tools were said to have been taken to her home. Other items such as the lawn mower, photocopier, and scanner had disappeared. Once again, Moloi felt the need to defend herself. "I do indeed have several items of school property in my home. They are there for reasons of security. You all know that the school is not adequately secure and that the storerooms are full. I have told staff members that these items are at my home, and if any are needed I will bring them to school as you let me know. As for the disappearance of items, some have been taken in for repairs. The school does not have enough money to get them back. You are certainly free to help raise the funds to get them back to the school!"

She wondered whether this meeting were ever going to end. What was this all about, anyway? She remembered that the SRC had indicated that she was too old to be a principal anymore and should be suspended. Had that sentiment spread to these other people who had her trapped in this room?

Then, another accusation, something about victimization. Moloi had reported a teacher to the PTSA for refusing to conduct more than thirty-two classes a week. That teacher, a SADTU member, considered this to be victimization. All Moloi could say was that she wanted the pupils taught and that no amount of persuasion would bring the teacher to take more classes. Communication between the two had broken down.

The meeting had turned into a marathon, and there seemed to be no way to end it. Finally, a commission of inquiry was suggested and everyone agreed that such a commission might be a way to resolve the issues raised. Moloi was not so sure. To her, the allegations being raised were nothing more that attempts by a small group of teachers to undermine her authority and force her out of the way. Already rumors were floating about the township that she was preparing to leave and that someone had already been selected to take her place. The SADTU teachers had gone so far as to pass a motion of no confidence in the principal.

The idea of an inquiry was truly unsettling—an insult, really. She wondered whether there might be some way to turn the situation around.

QUESTIONS FOR DISCUSSION

1. Describe the strategies used by SADTU leaders and others to advance their goals.
2. Why do you think Moloi was singled out for the protests and actions by the SADTU and other community persons?
3. Evaluate the communication strategies employed by those who were protesting Moloi and her administration.
4. If you were Moloi, how would you have handled the confrontational meetings set up for her? Justify.
5. If you were Moloi, what would you do or recommend now to resolve this crisis of leadership? Justify.

SELECTED BIBLIOGRAPHY

Allen, R. W., Madison, D. L., Porter, L. W., Renwich, P. A., & Mayes, B. T. (1979). Organizational politics: Tactics and characteristics of its actors. *California Management Review, 22,* 77–83.

Gudykunst, W. B., & Ting-Toomey, S. (1988). *Culture and interpersonal communication.* Newbury Park, CA: Sage.

Hofstede, G. (1991). *Cultures and organizations: Software of the mind.* London: McGraw-Hill.

Kipnis, D., Schmidt, D. M., & Wilkinson, I. (1980). Intraorganizational influence tactics: Explorations in getting one's way. *Journal of Applied Psychology, 65,* 440–452.

Mumby, D. K. (1988). *Communication and power in organizations: Discourse, ideology and domination.* Norwood, NJ: Ablex.

Preston, J., Du Toit, L., and Barger, I. (1998). *A potential model of transformational change applied to South Africa in research in organizational change and development,* Vol. 9 (R. Woodman & W. Pasmore Eds.). Greenwich, CT: JAI.

CASE 16

INTERCULTURAL PROBLEMS AT TOYO TRUE*

Tom McNutt

As he settled in his airline seat for the long leg of his ride back to Massachusetts, Scott Patjens tried hard to relax. Mentally exhausted from his four days in Tokyo and Yokohama, however, he could not rest.

To say that Patjens was perplexed and disappointed would be to give him credit for being in far greater control than he felt. The events of the past four days tumbled through his mind. He could not entirely dismiss the images, nor his feelings of discomfort. It was his nature to feel positive about his work and his efforts, but he could not feel at ease about this trip. Since his requested meeting just three hours ago with Merton Robinson, a western marketing executive who had lived in Japan for years, Patjens now understood some of the reasons why this trip had been unsettling for him. The entire situation was inconclusive, and many questions remained to be answered, not the least of which was whether or not he would be able to recover from the shaky start in his relationship with the Japanese group.

Patjens was the international training manager for True Boards, Inc., a worldwide producer and distributor of silicon chips and assembled printed circuit boards. His office was part of a larger corporate training program, that insiders affectionately called the "True U." The corporation had extensive international operations, with Toyo True, its Japanese subsidiary, the third most productive division in sales and revenue. Toyo True employed more than three hundred people and during the past year was responsible for corporate revenues exceeding $500 million. Initially

*All proper names, including that of the author, have been changed to protect individual identities.

part of the International Division of True Boards (InterTrue), the Japanese group had been so successful and become so large that the company had spun it off into a subsidiary. InterTrue, comprising all of the company's international operations except North American and Western European ventures, had provided a large percentage of its resources to Toyo True, which rightly had demanded its proportionate share. In the year since the spin-off of the Japanese group, however, the international division had rapidly developed other priorities and was no longer an internal resource for Toyo True. Toyo True, in reality, was on its own. Without a corporate support organization, it had the challenge of cultivating new relationships and channels to access corporate funding and service support, which it was now trying to rely upon heavily. Likewise, corporate officers were reassessing relationships and had developed initiatives to see how they could best handle the new structure. Those efforts were the reason Patjens had gone to Japan on this trip.

Patjens was now able to reflect on the reasons why his mission had mixed results. He now could recognize that several internal and external environmental conditions had heightened the difficulties that made smooth relationships between Toyo True and its corporate parent harder to achieve.

First, like much of the industry, True Board's rapid growth and success had literally outpaced its ability to develop an effective, working company infrastructure on a U.S. scale alone, much less to develop efficiently on a global frame.

Second, few of the corporate founders and current top management "had any clue," as they themselves put it, about Japanese business practices specifically, and they knew even less about Japanese cultural patterns. Two of Toyo True's officers were due to be placed on the board of directors, but that had not yet occurred. The feeling was that the company needed Japanese nationals to really run Toyo True, and had organized the subsidiary with Japanese officers in nearly every staffing position. Consequently, expectations and perceptions on both sides of the relationship were yet to be shared and had frequently been out of line.

Third, some corporate groups in the recent past had considered it an honor to work with Toyo True; but when they realized what a demanding commitment that was, with little actual glory associated with it (which they had been after), those same corporate-level personnel usually dropped out. As a result, few people in the corporation could claim direct experience working with the successful Japanese division.

Fourth, Toyo True officers knew full well how significant their role was in producing revenue for the parent company. Thus, it was their serious and intense feeling that corporate support should flow naturally to them without much effort on their part. They expected a great deal more attention and assistance than they had received and were disturbed that it had not been forthcoming.

Now, riding at thirty-seven thousand feet above the Pacific, headed for his Seattle connecting flight home, Patjens could reflect more objectively on his own efforts on this trip, well intentioned but apparently with questionable results. Corinne Lacey, one of his corporate associates, had laid the groundwork for the meetings and had been his "sponsor," seeing that he was included in the sessions dealing with training. The initial meetings, though cordial, had settled nothing. The Training Council meeting had been the largest, the most significant, and the most frustrating for Patjens. Corporate's objective for this meeting was to form a group of Toyo's senior managers who would meet regularly to determine training objectives and make recommendations for implementing them. The council membership primarily consisted of "functional" managers in technical areas such as customer service, systems engineering, and information resources. Nontechnical areas such as sales, marketing, finance, and human resources were also represented but were not a council priority.

Patjen's official role at the meeting was to represent corporate and to offer insight into how other international divisions managed their training. His unofficial role was to ensure that the council made a good start as a reliable communication and information source. He also wanted to convince the group to assign someone to work with corporate on training issues. A major concern to Patjens was that in all of Toyo True only one person had a job title with "training" implicit in it and that was a young woman who was a junior employee.

Patjens had several reasons for being nervous going into the meeting. He knew that most of the members were not sold on the need for this council and the extra work it promised for each of them. Additionally, his (and corporate's) main connection with this group of managers was the director of human resources (HR), who chaired the meeting. The worry was that the HR director was not credible with the other senior managers, yet corporate had to honor that formal connection. The final concern was Patjen's associate, Corinne Lacey. She was a real asset because she had been raised in Japan, knew Japanese customs, and spoke Japanese fluently. In spite of those attributes, however, Scott was unsure how she would be accepted because she was half African American and half Japanese in addition to being female.

Because Lacey was there, Patjens agreed to having the meeting conducted entirely in Japanese (although that rendered him practically useless). Lacey leaned over to translate critical items, and Patjens had to admit that helped a great deal. He knew the meeting structure, so he followed by watching and listening for nonverbal reactions. The major difficulty that occurred was when one key manager distanced himself from any training responsibility.

As he reflected again on that meeting, Patjens was still feeling some embarrassment about the surprise, impromptu presentation for which he had been volunteered by the HR director. He had been asked to share something about technical training. At True U. "technical" meant specific types of subjects, so Patjens gave the outlook on training in systems engineering. Unfortunately, as he was later told, technical training at Toyo True was anything but employee development, so the council members sat politely through the whole thing, probably wondering why so many valid training areas were being ignored. Another faulty assumption that caused awkward moments...

What almost surprised Patjens was that the net results from the meeting were positive. If this visit achieved long-term value, he could see how Lacey's work would be a major factor in ultimate successes. Managers left the meeting realizing that they were going to have to commit time, personnel, and financial resources to training. Patjens knew, though, that many of the members had serious reservations about the viability of the council—with nothing overtly mentioned, of course. The event was a victory of sorts, and that allowed moving further ahead.

What still bothered Patjens, though, was that the meeting closed with no conclusions drawn or assignments made. He was used to public discussion and debate, differences warmly brought out in a group session, not the energetic arguing that, he understood now, would yet be taking place at Toyo's offices. If only he or others had taken the time to consult someone like Merton Robinson earlier, they might have profited immensely from his years of living in the Far East and working with a variety of Japanese businesses and businessmen. So with those lingering frustrations, Patjens found that he was still stinging from the session with Robinson, recalling some of their exchange:

Robinson: What can I say, Scott. You simply had too many things designed and planned wrong.

Patjens: I know I didn't connect with them. They are probably writing up a blistering report and sending it home well ahead of me. I expect I will have to explain when I get home tomorrow. Specifically, though, where did we go wrong in our assumptions?

Robinson: First, I'll tell you what you did right, the things that kept those sessions from totally disintegrating, and that makes me think you can still recover. You did make the effort to take your own intercultural relations mini course, with the culture grams and all. You came with gifts, with proper greetings, and attention to the formalities. If I can believe your account of building some personal friendships, including that skilled performance of you and your chopsticks at the sushi bar, apparently you won a lot of points there. Also, you didn't rush into the business part. Those are all to the positive side.

Patjens: For which I should be grateful, I know. Then where did I go wrong?

Robinson: When you *did* get "down to business." The people at Toyo True still have little evidence that they are valued by corporate. Think back on how you approached that first business session.

Patjens: I simply did what we had determined we had to do here, what we so often have to do at other corporate locations. We honestly need more insight on how they see their needs, on how they wish us to help in the training end. Our approach was to be respectful of their situation and not claim to know all the answers. I still don't know why everything chilled so fast, and got colder in a hurry. I'm used to taking time to do a needs assessment and through that, building good relationships, not chilling them.

Robinson: That's where the up-front planning and assessment were faulty in this case, Scott. These people are accomplished professionals used to success. However, they want to do even better. They look for more resources and support from corporate levels, and they don't see it incidentally. Then here you come in and ask, "How can we help you?"

Patjens: What's wrong with that? That first meeting was with a sales manager and a person responsible for coordinating sales training. I was there to discuss what they were currently doing and to see if anything offered in the U.S. could be translated and localized to meet their needs. A lot of the True Boards–specific technical training that we have developed is very important and impossible to get anywhere else. What they do here in Japan is take our materials, translate them, and present them in an informal way. They get the essence of what we offer, but they miss a lot of the finer and more technical points. I really wanted them to understand how critical the corporate-specific details were, so I asked them how we could best do that. So I still wonder, what is wrong with that?

Robinson: Nothing, except you should have assessed those things, thoroughly, *before* coming here. You represent corporate, and they expected you to come here from a position of knowledge and strength, with an assessment done and a list of options or recommendations from which they could choose. Did you provide options or directions? They expected the resources to be committed to aid them.

Patjens: As a matter of fact, yes, I did have recommendations. I was here to offer them the name and address of a company in Japan that has taken proven U.S.-based selling skills programs and adapted them for the Japanese market. I am not sure if they knew about this offering, so I wanted to alert them to it. Their solution currently is to use some of the large training vendors who have been operating in Japan. While acceptable, this option is far from what we see as the cutting edge for us specifically.

Robinson: That first meeting couldn't have been so terribly bad. It led to other sessions, right?

Patjens: Actually, we ended up having what I still think was a reasonably decent meeting, even though there were many difficult moments because we didn't have a translator. When the inevitable misunderstandings occurred, we obviously did not connect on the language side. I am totally sure that I do not know how to read their nonverbal side. So, more confusion. They seemed to be fairly clear on why I was here, although I am not certain; thus, I did have to spend time selling them on why they should take time out of their day and week to struggle through a meeting with this blond guy from Massachusetts who cannot speak their language. When we were finally able to discuss their interest in technical training, it was clear to me that what they were currently doing was better than waiting for us, maybe, to find a way to translate and adapt for them. If training is not provided for them in Japanese, it is useless to them. On top of the language differences, too, are the cultural differences, which make selling and training approaches used in the U.S. irrelevant at best and offensive at the worst.

Robinson: How did they respond to your recommendation about the company already here?

Patjens: It appeared as though my endorsement of the skill-based program recently adapted for the Japanese markets was of genuine interest to them. I say, appeared, because I never heard that directly from anyone. I really felt in a delicate position, as it was hard for me to articulate the sensitive message that this was a suggestion only. We were not presuming to tell them what they should do, as if we knew. This was merely a gesture of goodwill that they could use if they saw fit. I was never really sure if they understood this point, though. As far as I could tell, I think they thought I was a decent enough person, but I sure have no idea if they think my presence will ever be of value in the future.

Robinson: And you are not likely to hear their direct response or their assurance that they understand, Scott. The Japanese are frequently painfully polite even if they hate a suggestion or are severely confused. Don't ever forget that their interpersonal style is far less direct than the typical Western approach. And don't sell yourself short on what you might have accomplished. You come all this way and you expect decisions made and directions settled. Those are very likely invalid expectations to bring here.

Patjens: I can see some of these things now! It has been obvious to us that anything developed by our organization was prepared with the

West in mind only. We have had some success in Hong Kong and Singapore with localizing our products, so we thought there might be a chance that some things could be localized immediately for Japan. If somebody from headquarters had spent more advance time with you, for instance, maybe we could have had a much better idea of how to come in more slowly and yet strongly.

Robinson: They expected leadership and strength, Scott, and they perceived corporate's unpreparedness and weakness. They believe that Toyo True is critical enough to the company's business that it deserves nothing less than a team of people, on site, working to solve its problems.

Patjens: What they got was one guy from corporate who may or may not ever come back, asking a lot of questions that he may or may not address. Oh, yeah, and since I let them know I have the rest of Asia, Eastern Europe, and Latin America in my territory, I suppose they perceived less than overwhelming commitment to them.

Robinson: They expected answers and money committed, but they received more questions and not even promises of financing beyond your "we'll have to determine the level of corporate money that can be allotted."

Patjens: But nobody in True Boards receives money automatically. Those are not realistic expectations. I've learned a lot this week, but know that I'm still pretty naive about how to work with this division. I can't help feeling, though, that the folks at Toyo True are also naive to expect things to fall into place so easily, in their way pressuring us into a win–lose posture. You know we're so tightly leveraged that funds for any project are hard to come by.

Robinson: I know that, yes, and the leaders at Toyo True have received the reports. But they do not understand that the division bringing in a large percentage of the revenue for the company has to compete with everyone else for scarce resources. They expect reward for accomplishment.

Such were the reflections and thoughts of Scott Patjens as he headed home. So, now, flying high but feeling low, he determined that as disturbing as this trip had been for him, he would see the success of the effort through. He was still wondering if learning experiences had to be so unsettling.

QUESTIONS FOR DISCUSSION

1. Identify the behaviors of the Japanese hosts that created frustrations for Scott Patjens. Identify as well the actions by Patjens or his corporate sponsors that created confusion or disappointment for the Toyo True managers.

2. Why should those actions cause difficulty?
3. Why is it difficult to observe differences, to interpret behaviors neutrally, to withhold judgment?
4. Specifically, what could Patjens and his corporate team have done to avoid the faulty assumptions, awkward and embarrassing situations, and frustrations?
5. What follow-up actions should Patjens take upon his return to the home office? What recommendations should he direct to corporate training people? To Toyo True's managers? Justify your response using researched intercultural communication principles.

SELECTED BIBLIOGRAPHY

Chen, G. (1989). Relationships of the dimensions of intercultural communication competence. *Communication Quarterly, 37,* 118–133.

Goodyear, F. H., & West, A. (1977). An organizational framework for cross cultural communication. *Southern Communication Journal, 42,* 178–190.

Johnson, J. D., & Tims, A. R. (1985). Communication factors related to closer international ties. *Human Communication Research, 12,* 259–273.

McCroskey, J. C., & Richmond, V. P. (1990). Willingness to communicate: Differing cultural perspectives. *Southern Communication Journal, 56,* 72–77.

Shuter, R. (1990). The centrality of culture. *Southern Communication Journal, 55,* 237–249.

Thiederman, S. (1991). *Bridging cultural barriers for corporate success: How to manage the multicultural work force.* Lexington, MA: Lexington.

Toomey, S. (1988). Rhetorical sensitivity style in three cultures: France, Japan, and the United States. *Communication Studies, 39,* 28–36.

SAN FRANCISCO BANK

Stewart L. Tubbs

Andrew J. Hanna (Andy to all his associates) is a senior loan officer at the San Francisco Bank, an agricultural bank with an annual loan volume exceeding $200 million. Hanna is one of twenty loan officers in the bank's credit department. He services accounts totaling more than $10 million in outstanding loans. This is more than most of the other senior loan officers handle. He has a degree in business, a law degree, and more than ten years of banking experience. His background and experience are widely acknowledged throughout the bank and frequently noted by the banking industry in the area as well.

One evening last January, because of his responsibility for a client's loan, Hanna was required to attend a board meeting of that company's agricultural accounts. The firm was located in a different city, thus requiring a three-hour drive merely to get to the meeting. The meeting started promptly at 7:00 P.M. and was scheduled to end at 9:30. However, board business and deliberations extended the meeting until 11:30. Hanna was required to remain throughout the entire session. Although tired and authorized to stay overnight, Hanna decided to save the bank the expense of a hotel room and breakfast and drove home to San Francisco, arriving at about 3:00 A.M.

The next morning at 7:50 A.M. (five minutes after normal starting time at the San Francisco Bank), Peter Prince, bank president, made his customary walk through bank offices. He noted that Andrew Hanna was not at work. He asked Hanna's secretary, Melinda Davis, "Miss Davis, would you please check Mr. Hanna's travel log to see where he might be to explain his absence this morning?" Davis hurriedly consulted the travel notebook but could find no reference about Hanna traveling on this day. She reported, "I'm sorry, Mr. Prince, but all I can locate is Mr. Hanna's attending a board meeting in Madera yesterday evening. He was scheduled to be here this morning, however." Prince then returned to John Jackson's desk, inquiring, "John, do you have any idea where Andy Hanna is this morning? His secretary doesn't know of anything except an early-evening board meeting in Madera last night. He should be here, and if he's not, then someone around here certainly ought to know why not."

Meanwhile, Hanna slept in and came to work at 10:00 A.M. Immediately after he checked in, his supervisor, John Jackson, came up to Andy's desk, asking, "Where were you this morning?" Hanna responded, "I was home in bed," and then went on to explain the events of the night before. Jackson told him that Prince had specifically noticed his absence when he made his morning rounds. "Andy, he made Melinda go through your travel log, and he was really upset when neither she nor I could shed any light on where you were. You and I had better talk about this after you've gone through your morning correspondence." And with that sharply worded comment, Jackson returned to his office. Hanna could see that Jackson was angry; apparently Prince was angry, and now, feeling unjustly accused of who-knew-what, Hanna himself was getting upset.

Later that morning, at Jackson's desk, the following dialogue occurred:

Jackson: Andy, you know you're expected to be in the bank, at your desk, by 7:45, regardless of the circumstances.

Hanna: I think that's bull, John. I was out until 3:00 in the morning on bank business, and I was also trying to save the bank the cost of a motel room and breakfast. I felt that my options were (1) call you at home at 11:30, when the meeting ended; or (2) call you at 3:00 A.M., when I got home, to tell you I would be late getting to work this morning; or (3) set the alarm for 7:45 to call in; or (4) spend the night in a motel, eat breakfast, and come in around 1:00 this afternoon; or (5) come into work with about two or three hours' sleep; or (6) do what I did by coming to work by 10:00.

Jackson: I don't care about all your options. You either get in here on time at 7:45, or you get a motel room and call in first thing in the morning explaining where you are and why.

Hanna: John, I manage $10 million worth of business, and you want me to report this level of detail? I can't believe I'm hearing this.

Jackson: Rules are rules, Andy, and they must be followed by everyone. We don't want any complaints about preferential treatment or special privileges.

Over a period of time, Hanna and the other loan officers decided informally to comply with the new "rule," to just go ahead and get a motel room and come into work at about 1:00 P.M. the day following an out-of-town late board meeting (which was a frequent occurrence with their business loans and range of clients in the northern California region).

The new practice now costs the San Francisco Bank an average of $100 additional per out-of-town trip. Jackson seems to be satisfied with this resolution, and so do the other bank officers.

QUESTIONS FOR DISCUSSION

1. What primary elements in this situation caused the conflict? What caused the conflict to escalate?
2. What would you do differently to improve the way this conflict was resolved?
3. What specific conflict management strategies and tactics could Jackson have used for a more satisfactory resolution? Hanna? Others at the bank?
4. What steps would you recommend to the San Francisco Bank to help the officers avoid similar situations from occurring in the future?

SELECTED BIBLIOGRAPHY

Conrad, C. (1983). Power, performance and supervisors' choice of strategies of conflict management. *Western Journal of Speech Communication, 47,* 218–228.

O'Barr, W. M. (1984). Asking the right questions about language and power. In C. Kramarae, M. Schulz, & W. M. O'Barr (Eds.), *Language and power* (pp. 260–280). Beverly Hills, CA: Sage.

Renwick, P. (1975). Perception and management of superior–subordinate conflict. *Organizational Behavior and Human Performance, 13,* 444–456.

Robbins, S. P. (1978). "Conflict management" and "conflict resolution" are not synonymous terms. *California Management Review, 21,* 67–75.

Thomas, K. W. (1976). Conflict and conflict management. In M. D. Dunnette (Ed.), *The Handbook of Industrial and Organizational Psychology.* Chicago: Rand McNally.

Vroom, V. H., & Yetton, P. W. (1973). *Leadership and decision making.* Pittsburgh: University of Pittsburgh Press.

HEARTHSTONE HOMES
Thomas E. Schillar

Hearthstone Homes began in the late 1960s when Ed Stone became general partner of his own construction firm after years of profitable experience in the housing industry. In the 1950s Stone had worked as a framing carpenter on the Levittown, New York, housing project. Levittown had begun immediately after World War II, with 450 homes by 1946, and 60,000 by the late 1950s. As one of the early planned communities, Levittown sported mass-produced homes, with the much talked-about look-alike frames, differing only by color of paint or shingles. Stone, however, early developed an appreciation for mass-produced housing and was able to apply that experience and interest in developing his own company. Shortly after the start of Hearthstone Homes on the West Coast, Stone was heavily involved in the marketing side of his construction business. When modular housing became a strong force in the housing industry in the early 1980s, Stone developed a manufacturing facility in Renton, Washington, and began to pursue, profitably, this new market niche.

Bob Bennet had worked in the modular housing industry for seven years, the last four with Hearthstone Homes. For Stone, Bennet had first been a coordinator for site selection and development, where he earned a reputation with corporate management as an effective manager and as an up-and-coming leader. Although his current position with the company paid fairly well, Bennet felt that his next step with Hearthstone should be in the marketing division, perhaps as manager of one of the company's nine retail sales offices.

In late summer of 1990, Stone, as president of Hearthstone Homes, discussed the newly created position of sales manager in the Spokane, Washington, office with Bennet. After many meetings and much discussion about potential, Bennet was appointed to that position and was assigned a new office in a suburban area close to the downtown city core.

Bennet's first few months on the job in Spokane were hectic but challenging and, somehow, even pleasurable. His initial task was to develop a sales force consisting of three sales associates and then to provide the training necessary to make them productive. To Bennet, this was a difficult though rewarding task, and he was pleased with his selection of the sales crew to work with him.

Maurice Martin, forty-six, had worked in housing sales for almost twenty years. His initial experience in the industry was as a mobile home salesperson with a large dealership. Martin started his own dealership but after several years went out of business because he lacked the skills to build capital and manage the company's finances. Within a short time he became the top sales volume producer in Hearthstone Homes' Spokane office and remained the leader in most monthly periods.

A second associate selected by Bennet was Leanne Diehl, thirty-six. Diehl had worked, with moderate success, as a real estate agent for several years with the P. L. Curtis Real Estate Group in the Spokane area. She was selected to work with Hearthstone because she seemed to know the Spokane metropolitan area better than any other person Bennet had interviewed. Diehl had disliked having to put in "floor time" in the Medical Lake office for Curtis. She appreciated the extensive personal contact nature of the work with Hearthstone.

The final member of the Spokane Hearthstone team was John Backstrom, thirty-five, who joined the sales group early in 1991. Backstrom had successfully been involved in advertising sales in Seattle, and the move to Hearthstone Homes was a complete career shift for him. To date, he has not produced a great deal in sales ("Still learning the ropes," he would say), but Bennet had used, and paid for, his advertising background and experience.

The sales team seemed to be working together very well, in spite of having different personality types and taking very different approaches to selling in the housing market. The team's success came even in the face of a downturn in general real estate and a soft market for all forms of housing. In the fall of 1990, with input from Stone and corporate officers at Hearthstone headquarters in the Puget Sound region, and with consensus from the Spokane sales force, the following goals/projections were established:

Sales Goals

October	$230,000	January	260,000
November	230,000	February	260,000
December	245,000	March	275,000

Meeting just a few days after the close of March, when both monthly and six-month figures had been compiled, the Spokane sales team reviewed actual sales figures for the period. Bennet began, "We have all followed our production figures for the last several months, and I know you are aware of where we are. With March deals all figured in, this is how the actual sales look in comparison with Hearthstone's projections:

Actual Sales

October	$242,000	January	235,000
November	227,000	February	272,000
December	218,000	March	238,000

"I might add," Bennet continued, "that these were our goals as well. I don't need to say it has been disappointing overall. We've had some successes in a couple of the months, but I really felt that we were realistic in our goals and that we would reach them."

Diehl responded quickly, saying, "Bob, you know how hard we've worked. This is not a lazy or incompetent group. In light of the economy around here—you know, the layoffs at Alcoa, the rising unemployment overall, the downturn in downtown—I personally think we've done very well."

Martin added, "I agree. With the exception of the last few weeks, I've felt very good about my own production. When things are this tight, nobody moves fast; but I'm betting on more reductions in interest rates and the loosening up of money for some of those who are planning to build—the developers as well as individual contractors. I have those three deals you know about, all pending, which alone could double the whole past six months."

Bennet, trying to brighten and be positive with his team, replied, "I know, Maurice. I'm personally very positive about the direction we're going. I just hope Ed Stone and the guys in Seattle don't pull the plug on us. I know Ed's disappointed. He told me so during last week's phone report. Said he expected more from me."

Backstrom added, "Bob, doesn't he know how much you've put into this office? I've never known anyone with so many good ideas for marketing, especially for a product like our modular home construction, which answers so many needs right now. I've appreciated the way you have involved us all, how we've worked together, and how we've drawn on all our skills to set a lot of things in motion that have never been done around here. Hearthstone surely knows all the things we've started; surely Ed knows how the economy has been here in the Inland Empire. I cannot think for a moment he'd close the office or anything so drastic. So we're short a few thousand in projections. I'm satisfied, and you've told us you are satisfied with our progress, too."

Bennet's answer was quick: "I am. I am. It's just that I'm starting to get signals that somebody, or something, in Seattle is working on Stone to convince him he made a mistake in setting me up here. That was his decision, and he pulled for me. Hey, I don't think I'm paranoid or anything, OK? I just don't want all your work, and my work, of these past months to be disregarded. Or, what could be worse, wasted. Let's keep on it—tie some of these deals together. We have to make up some ground this month. I can feel it!"

Less than a week later, on April 10, Ed Stone placed an emergency call to Bob Bennet in Spokane. Stone did the talking. "Bob, I've just been reviewing in some detail your latest figures. I expected the Spokane area to produce a lot more action than what you and your crew have produced in the last six months. I'm sending a consultant over to work with you and your staff next Monday morning. He's my top guy on this side of the mountains, and I'm hoping that he can bring your group alive."

At precisely 8:00 A.M. on Monday, Stewart Plotz, the consultant, arrived at the Hearthstone Homes office to meet with Bennet and his staff. Bennet, Diehl, and Backstrom were there to greet him. However, Martin failed to arrive until 8:45. Frankly, there were some tense, chilly moments when Martin walked in. "Sorry I'm late. Hope I haven't held up the start of the meeting. I had three morning appointments I'd made before this session was scheduled. I was able to change a couple of them but felt I needed to keep the third so I hustled there and kept it as short as I could."

Plotz was unmoved. "Mr. Martin, I don't know you, and I have to figure you think you had legitimate reasons to run your morning errands. All I'm going to say now is to remind you that this is your job; and if Ed Stone is going to lay out the money for my time and fly me all the way over here to eastern Washington, you'd better remember it's your job. I would suggest to you three observations: item 1, there was no good excuse for being late to a meeting of such importance to this sales center; item 2, although you have an acceptable sales record, in the last six weeks you've not written one contract; and item 3, you might be big stuff in this office, but your record is very average compared to sales associates in some of our other regions. Now that should be clear and behind us. Let's get on with this review."

"This review" was a full-day, detailed check of the Spokane office's overall performance. Bennet provided information, answered questions, and tried to give explanations. Any attempt to describe what was in progress was dismissed as a "copout" or as "promises, promises." Bennet's sales associates were uncommonly quiet. Plotz finished with some superficial suggestions on how to make more sales, with little response and no questions from the associates. He said good-bye to Bennet, promised to return in a month to review the office's progress, and left to catch the shuttle flight back to Seattle. When Bennet said his farewell to Plotz at his rental car, he went back into the office only to find it empty—no notes, no papers, only an uneasy silence.

The next morning Martin, Diehl, and Backstrom called Bennet to request a meeting with him. When they arrived, Martin was visibly upset and said to his manager, "Bob, I like and respect you a great deal for what you've given us here. But I am not going to take the kind of abuse that hotshot gave me yesterday. I've produced a lot of sales volume from scratch for this company, and I don't expect to be treated that way by him or you or anyone else." The words came rapidly as Martin furrowed his brow and added, "If you can't correct this quick, I'll go to work for someone else." Diehl and Backstrom nodded and mumbled their agreement, mostly looking down at the floor in front of them. Naturally Bennet was stunned, and he said so, adding, "Come on back tomorrow morning, when we've all had a chance to reflect on this and to cool down." There were no objections, and the sales team seemed relieved to be gone from the office.

Late into the evening, Bennet sat alone in his office asking himself what to do. He had keyboarded at least six lists and scenarios into the computer, printed them out, looked at them, and tossed all into the recycle box. All he could think about was the six months of hard work that were about to go down the drain.

QUESTIONS FOR DISCUSSION

1. Conflicts are natural in any organization. What would you do to try to understand the causes of this conflict? Are the causes and solutions strictly within Bennet's group?
2. In what ways was Ed Stone responsible for this conflict? How can he be, or should he be, involved in its resolution?
3. What specific steps can Bob Bennet take to ensure that this conflict is resolved effectively and to minimize the recurrence of similar incidents? Do you think Bennet will keep his team?
4. If you had been Bennet, would you have allowed the consultant to treat your sales associates the way they were treated? What risks were there to Bennet?

SELECTED BIBLIOGRAPHY

Infante, D. A., & Gorden, W. I. (1985). Superiors' argumentativeness and verbal aggressiveness as predictors of subordinates' satisfaction. *Human Communication Research, 12,* 117–125.
Jablin, F. M. (1979). Superior–subordinate communication: The state of the art. *Psychological Bulletin, 86,* 1201–1222.

Jablin, F. M. (1980). Superior's upward influence, satisfaction, and openness in superior–subordinate communication: A re-examination of the Pelz effect. *Human Communication Research, 6,* 210–220.

Mellinger, G. D. (1956). Interpersonal trust as a factor in communication. *Journal of Abnormal and Social Psychology, 52,* 304–309.

Sanford, A. C., Hunt, G. T., & Bracey, H. J. (1976). *Communication behavior in organizations.* Columbus, OH: Merrill/Prentice Hall.

Wheeless, L. R., Wheeless, V. E., & Howard, R. D. (1984). The relationships of communication with supervisor and decision participation to employee job satisfaction. *Communication Quarterly, 32,* 222–232.

NEW RUSSIAN SCHOOL

Communicating in a Changing Organizational Environment

Barbara Mae Gayle and Elayne Shapiro

BACKGROUND

Mary and John Owens had spent considerable time in Russia early in their careers as American diplomats. They both learned the language and adopted many of the customs. It was not surprising that the Owenses wanted their daughter, Nicole, to speak Russian even though they now resided in the United States.

All of Jackie and Vince Voltz's relatives were from Russia. Only Vince and Jackie and his brother, Joseph, and his wife, Anne, were living in the United States. Now that Vince and Jackie's son, Aaron, and Joseph and Anne's daughter, Suzanne, were preschool age, both families wanted a Russian immersion school experience for their children.

When two other families from church, Gustov and Thelma Wilkes and Charles and Lillian Howard, expressed interest in having their sons attend a Russian immersion school and mentioned their friends, the Owenses, a coalition was formed to investigate the possibilities. A phone call to the leading School of Foreign Languages revealed that no Russian language immersion program existed. But as the director of public relations, Shelia Hartwick, explained, the school was contemplating adding both a Japanese and a Russian preschool program. In fact, Shelia herself had urged the Russian program be started because she wanted her own four-year-old daughter, Emma, and her three-year-old son, Emile, to learn Russian.

A meeting was set up with school leaders that week, and plans were made to begin a Russian immersion preschool in the fall. Talk centered around a second-floor location in a bright sunny room and the hiring of a most impressive teacher, Trina Nicholson. Fees were set, and all seven children were enrolled in preschool classes for fall.

When school opened in the fall, the parents were flabbergasted. The fees had increased substantially, and the assigned classroom was in the basement of the building. The Japanese program was given the second-floor room and was highly promoted even though the Russian immersion program had attracted another five children. By Christmas, the Voltzes, Owenses, Wilkeses, and Howards were discussing operating their own program. As Joseph claimed, "Look, we have two lawyers, a physician, an accountant, a CEO, and a professor. We have the talent to start this organization, and it has already almost doubled in size."

In April a building was identified that would house the "New Russian School," and plans were being made for a summer session. Shelia expressed a desire to be director of the school, telling the parental planning group how her ideas for the Russian immersion program had been denied or altered from the start at the School of Foreign Languages. It was agreed to hire her as director, and John Owens (a successful businessman), Gustov Wilkes (a lawyer), Jackie Voltz (a physician), Joseph Voltz (a professor), and Lillian Howard (an accountant) agreed to serve as the board of directors. In that capacity, Lillian recruited their current preschool teacher, Trina, to be their Russian teacher.

By the end of May, all twelve children had signed up for the summer school, and the weekly noon meetings of the board of directors had resulted in a building lease, insurance, a hired teacher, a hired director, a fee schedule, and an operating budget.

THE NEW SCHOOL

When summer session began with twenty-two children enrolled, the board of directors faced their first crisis. Unbeknown to them, Shelia had been busy actively promoting the New School and its facilities, but she had been unable to locate a teacher for the last four weeks of the term when Trina took her annual trip to Russia. The board members felt obligated with other families enrolled to provide a full summer session instead of the minisession they had planned around Trina's schedule. They also did not like the new teacher, Luke, whom Shelia had hired. He was dictatorial and abrasive.

By the time the summer session was halfway completed, the board had located another teacher, Kristen, to teach the three-year-old class in the fall, and Shelia had hired two teacher's aides. Enrollment for the fall increased to thirty students, fifteen in Kristen's class and fifteen in Trina's four-year-old class. The insurance policy had to be renegotiated and more building space rented. Lillian talked about the happy problems Shelia's public relations abilities had created, while Gustov and Jackie worried about growing too fast.

Board meetings were held bimonthly. Everyone shared tasks, and Shelia often met with the board. Decisions to purchase the extra equipment needed for the increased enrollments were weighed against salary considerations for the teacher's aides. Talk focused on keeping the school solvent and stable.

At the December meeting, Shelia reported that six new families would be joining the school during the winter term. She chatted happily about the nice families and the eight new children. Board members were in shock. Joseph asked where Shelia planned to place these children. Shelia said, "Five will join the four-year-old class, and three will join the three-year-old class." Jackie reminded Shelia that Trina was already concerned that the classes were too large. Shelia suggested they have a mixed class and hire Luke, claiming, "after all, he really did fine this summer." In the end, the board members suggested Shelia advertise for another teacher and clean out the room currently being used as a storeroom to house the new class.

At the next meeting, Shelia was absent because of her involvement in the extensive Christmas celebration she had planned for the school. Kristen appeared and asked to speak to the board. She said she loved her class but all the extra planning for Shelia's extravagances demanded more of her free time than she could devote, so she was resigning January 15 when the new term was to begin. The board pleaded with her to stay, and Kristen conceded as long as her role in the spring raffle and the May Day festivals was a minor one. Because the board knew nothing of either event, they guaranteed Kristen that her class would be smaller and her workload less arduous.

After Kristen left, the board members lamented about Shelia's lack of communication and her overenthusiastic plans. "Yet," Lillian cautioned, "the school is thriving both financially and academically." "But I hate constantly renegotiating for the insurance and building space," claimed John. Jackie, however, worried about how to split the classes to accommodate the new teacher, Barbara, and the existing children who were already assigned to Kristen or Trina. Gustov suggested letting Trina make those decisions, and so the new term found the eight new children and four of the slowest learners in Barbara's class, and a mixture of thirteen three- and four-year-olds in Trina's and Kristen's classes. As the winter term progressed, the board ironed out facility and equipment demands but were bombarded by plans for Shelia's fund-raising raffle. Her complaints about how much work it was for her and how little the teachers helped fell on deaf ears. Both accolades for Shelia's responsiveness with the parents and complaints about her demands on the teachers reached the board of directors.

During the spring term, the board decided to add another member as they were overwhelmed and unable to fulfill all the duties that were necessary to run the school. Carol Hull, a new parent and graduate student, was asked to participate. When the board met in March, Trina reported that she was looking into a master's teaching program that would enhance her credentials. She reported that she might not be able to teach the following year because of her class schedule. Immediately, the board agreed to work around her classes and hold her preschool Russian immersion class in the afternoon or morning to keep her. Trina suggested the board hire her to teach the kindergarten class they were adding in the fall, and she would concentrate her coursework in either the morning or afternoon hours. It was agreed, and, after Trina left, the board discussed how fortunate they were to have such a high-quality teacher. Shelia suggested that if need be, the school could replace Trina: "What's important is that we try to maintain both preschool and kindergarten classes next year."

BIGGER PROBLEMS EMERGE

In late April, the board was planning for the summer session. Shelia told them she enrolled another four children into the program. Trina told them she could not arrange her master's teaching classes to fit entirely into the morning or afternoon; therefore, she would be resigning after the summer session.

The board members met without Shelia to discuss how to retain Trina. They decided to offer her a director of teachers position because they wanted to keep her and she was much better at communicating with the other teacher than Shelia. When the board met with Trina, she accepted their offer. When Shelia saw the advertisement for two teachers, she assumed that Trina was leaving the school and was astounded when she learned Trina was going to be the director of teachers.

Shelia met with the board members to express her concerns. She asked how she fit into their plans. Although the board assured her they wanted to keep her, they were unclear as to how the school would be run. They told Shelia they expected her to do everything she was currently doing, but conducting the teachers' meetings and hiring teachers would be Trina's job. Shelia was visibly upset as she told them, "I will consider your offer."

Board members were confused, burned out, and discussed together their desire to keep both women. A short time later, Shelia sent them a written agreement requesting that she be a voting member of the board, and the overall director in charge, with Trina reporting directly to her. Otherwise, they could accept her resignation. Jackie revealed that Trina had confided in her that Shelia and Trina had had numerous small conflicts starting when they were both employed at the School of Foreign Language. Gustov reported that the New Russian School was a financial success and that eight additional families were expected to join next fall. Joseph asked, "Why hasn't anyone told me about more growth, about the conflict, and about the request?" After a very long meeting, board members decided to engage a consultant.

QUESTIONS FOR DISCUSSION

1. If you were called in as a communication consultant by the New Russian School, what kind of information would you want to gather in making your assessments?
2. What are the potential pitfalls facing this organization?
3. What, if anything, would you do about the conflict between Shelia and Trina? Between the board members and Shelia? What are some possible organizational structures you could recommend to the new school? How will these structures aid or inhibit communication among organizational members?
4. How can the board members, the director, the director of teachers, and the parents of students interact to create an organizational identity conducive to further growth and expansion?
5. Identify the various turning points in this organization that caused more problems than was originally recognized.

SELECTED BIBLIOGRAPHY

Bullis, C., & Bach, B. W. (1989). Socialization turning points: An examination of change in organizational identity. *Western Journal of Speech Communication.* 53, 273–293.

Daniels, T. D., & DeWine, S. (1991). Communication process as target and tool for consultancy intervention: Rethinking a hackneyed theme. *Journal of Educational and Psychological Consultation, 2,* 303–322.

Ellis, B. H. (1992). The effects of uncertainty and source credibility on attitudes about organizational change. *Management Communication Quarterly, 6,* 34–57.

Jablin, F. M. (1987). Formal organization structure. In F. M. Jablin (Ed.), *Handbook of organizational communication* (pp. 389–419). Newbury Park, CA: Sage.

McPhee, R. D. (1985). Formal structure and organizational communication. In R. D. McPhee & P. K. Tompkins (Eds.), *Organizational communication: Traditional themes and new directions* (pp. 149–177). Beverly Hills, CA: Sage.

Miller, K. I., & Monge, P. R. (1985). Social information and employee anxiety about organizational change. *Human Communication Research, 11,* 365–386.

A FRIEND IN NEED AND THE EXPLOSIVE BOSS

Diana W. Kincaid, Gerald D. Hamsmith, and Thomas D. Cavenagh

INTRODUCTION

Linda Slotki is a legal secretary at Harris, Tessler, and Brock, a fast-paced, competitive law firm in Chicago (referred to as HTB hereafter). HTB is fairly small, and the atmosphere is socially relaxed though professionally intense. The structure of HTB (which is apparent on the organizational chart depicted in Figure 20.1) is such that the name partners (Lenard Harris, Frank Tessler, and Sam Brock) have the most authority, though they share their decision-making and other powers with the senior partners in the firm. The second tier of partners, the nonequity partners, are next on the organizational ladder, followed by the associates and staff managers, then staff (including secretaries, paralegals, etc.). Regardless of this formal hierarchical structure, the name partners like to refer to the firm as "a family" and claim that each employee is valued as a person. The secretaries and attorneys often eat lunch together, share stories, and even tell off-color jokes. Though Slotki does not commonly use profanity, other employees at the firm use swear words occasionally (e.g., "What the ---- is this?" or "That's bull----").

Slotki has worked for the same attorney, Mike Russo, an associate of the firm for over five years. Russo works under a great deal of pressure (which sometimes sets off his temper), and he relies greatly on his secretary. Through their five years together, he has, at times, been less than satisfied with Slotki's work. He discussed problems with her as they arose but chose not to enter any official complaints into her employee file since he viewed her as a friend. Russo was especially patient when Slotki went through a divorce. She explained the problems with her work as

168

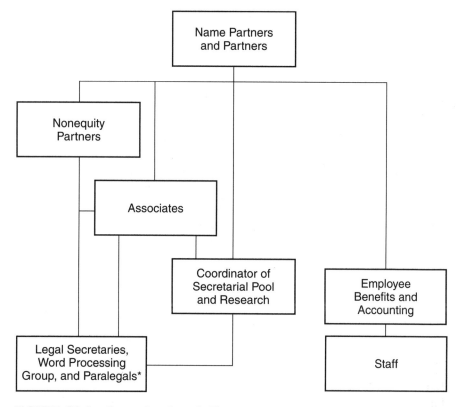

FIGURE 20.1   Organizational Chart

*This firm has a word-processing department that does overflow work as part of the secretarial pool. These secretaries do not work for any single lawyer on a long-term basis as legal secretaries do. All secretaries are theoretically accountable to the secretarial pool coordinator as well as the lawyer for whom they are working. The paralegal staff is also accountable to both the coordinator and the attorney in charge of the cases on which they are working.

temporary by-products of her troubled emotional state during several tearful sessions in Russo's office during which she vented her anger and depression about the breakup of her marriage. Russo provided free legal advice, tried to help the couple negotiate their divorce settlement, and finally referred the couple to a competent divorce lawyer. He did this all informally and without charge.

Throughout this time, Russo felt that Slotki's work was unsatisfactory. He often sought additional help from the secretarial pool that usually provided fill-in secretaries during the vacations and sick leaves of the legal secretaries or handled the overload of secretarial work for attorneys at trial. In an effort to explain why he seemed to be continually requesting additional help from the secretarial pool, he let the other secretaries know of his frustrations with Slotki's attitude (which he described as "lackadaisical at best").

PROBLEM

On one particularly harrowing day, Russo returned from court in an obvious rage. He called Slotki into his office and explained that she had typed the wrong courtroom number as well as the wrong address for the federal court building (an address that she had typed at least a hundred times before) on the official documents that he had needed to file that day. The judge was lenient but pointed out the mistake in front of a crowded courtroom in a sarcastic manner and severely embarrassed Russo. Russo was furious. Slotki considered this a small and simple mistake and was offended at Russo's tone. She responded by reminding him that it was his responsibility to proofread anything he signed. She then turned to leave his office and return to her desk outside. Russo did not consider their conversation finished and was so angry at her flippant response that he followed after her and threatened, "Next mistake like that and I am going to write you up" (putting a formal note in her employee file indicating some problem with her work). He then flipped the document into her "in" box to be retyped and refiled. "Don't throw things at me!" she retorted defiantly. "Just get it f---ing right this time!" he yelled back. Then he returned to his office to cool down and get back to work.

   As far as Russo was concerned, the whole thing was past and forgotten. His relationship with Slotki seemed back to normal by the end of the day, and the next day things were back to business as usual. But the coordinator of the secretaries, Tom Blair, had reported to Harris, the senior partner at the firm, that Slotki had complained about Russo's "verbal abuse and public humiliation" of the day before. The following week, Russo was called into Harris's office. He has no idea why. Then, Harris explained that this meeting was a formal reprimand for Russo's "unprofessional conduct" and, in particular, for his "use of profanity." A written reprimand would be included in his file (which was used annually by the partners to evaluate the associates to determine raises and promotions). Harris demanded that Russo formally apologize, refrain from ever using profanity in this office again, and address any further concerns he had with Slotki through the secretarial coordinator.

   Russo felt humiliated, but he was also extremely angry. Practically everyone at the firm used the kind of language he had used, and he had heard more than a few choice words come out of Slotki's own mouth when she was talking with him about her husband. Nevertheless, he apologized to her. He still felt unsettled about the whole situation. He felt betrayed by Slotki and a little nervous about how to speak with her after this episode. He made up his mind to speak to her no more than was absolutely necessary to get his work done.

Slotki felt vindicated, but her work continued to slide. She still regarded Russo as a close friend and even sought to confide in him about the problems she was facing as a newly divorced mother. Russo was unsympathetic. He tried hard to maintain a purely professional relationship and resisted all leads into a personal conversation. But Slotki continued to elaborate about her child care problems as an explanation for why she was continually leaving early or taking days off. She assured him that she would regain her focus once things settled down at home.

This situation was not only personally uncomfortable but also professionally crippling for Russo because his productivity was hampered by his lack of a competent secretary. The problems he had overlooked in the past were much more annoying to him now. However, after his previous reprimand, he was skittish about confronting Slotki over her absenteeism, excessive time on the phone, disregard for proper filing procedures, or any other work-related problem. He feared that anything he said would be regarded as a form of revenge for the letter in his file. He followed the instructions from Harris by calling these problems to the attention of Blair, the secretarial coordinator. Blair was unresponsive. Finally, exasperated, Russo requested a new secretary. Blair told him curtly, "There are no other secretaries. You'll have to either learn to work with Linda or write up the appropriate documentation to have her fired. That's the only way we can give you a new secretary."

Confidential facts: Slotki's perspective

As Russo was becoming less patient with her occasional mistakes, Slotki was feeling more unappreciated and getting increasingly annoyed at what she considered to be his continual overreactions to any tiny error. After all, she often put in overtime when he was on trial despite the fact that she had an eight-year-old son to care for. She also resented the hypocrisy she saw in Russo when he *agreed* with her that her own husband was a philanderer, yet he continued to use his maleness to fit into the old boys partnership by going to places like Hooters with the partners for lunch or after work. These types of lunches had long since replaced the lunches he used to have with her and the other secretaries or staff. Slotki felt that after five years of service, of pulling Mike's tail out of the fire when he needed it, she deserved a little respect.

Confidential facts: Russo's perspective

Russo was feeling more stress than usual this year because during his review this year, he would be considered for a promotion from associate to nonequity partner. Becoming a nonequity partner would provide Russo with a substantial raise, a chance to participate in major decisions facing the firm, an entertainment fund for courting clients, a new office with funds for Russo to decorate it personally to his liking, and other perks in addition to increased status in the firm. Becoming a nonequity partner was the next step toward becoming a senior partner. Senior partners got all the rewards of nonequity partners plus more, say, a bigger 401K package and a direct percentage of the firm's net profits each year. Russo was a little self-conscious this year because he knew his work would be reviewed carefully by Harris and the other partners. For this reason, his billable hours as well as the quality of his work were extremely important to him. What irritated Russo most was that he knew he could get more work done if he had a secretary who could keep up with him. He resented the fact that he had to go through the secretarial pool and beg whomever was around to stay late whenever he wanted to do any substantial work past 5 o'clock. Each time he did, he had to fill in the secretary on how certain documents should be filed or what his various abbreviations meant.

QUESTIONS FOR DISCUSSION

1. What formal and informal communication networks can you identify operating in this firm? What effect do these communication networks have on what is said to whom?
2. Using the organizational chart of the firm, describe how upward, downward, and horizontal communication operate in this case.
3. How does one evaluate and select among the outcomes available in a context involving conflict?
4. What are Russo's options in this case, and which are preferable?
5. How do people tend to communicate differently in contexts involving conflict?
6. How can communication be improved in contexts involving conflict?
7. What processes are available to employers and employees involved in conflict? What are the advantages and disadvantages of each?
8. What ethical issues exist in the confrontation between the lawyer and his secretary? Are any of these issues different because the lawyer is a member of a profession?

SELECTED BIBLIOGRAPHY

Bazerman, M. H., & Neale, M. A. (1992). *Negotiating rationally.* New York: Free Press.

Deal, T. E., & Kennedy, A. A. (1962). *Corporate cultures.* Reading, MA: Addison-Wesley.

Fisher, R., & Ury, W. (1981). *Getting to yes: Negotiating agreement without giving in* (2nd ed.). New York: Penguin.

Folger, J. P., Poole, M. S., & Stutman, R. K. (1997). *Working through conflict: Strategies for relationships, groups and organizations.* New York: Longman.

Kottler, J. A. (1994). *Beyond blame: A new way of resolving conflicts in relationships.* San Francisco: Jossey-Bass.

Kriteck, P. B. (1994). *Negotiating at an uneven table: Developing moral courage in resolving our conflicts.* San Francisco: Jossey-Bass.

Schermerhorn, J. R., Hunt, J. G., & Osborn, R. N. (1995). *Managing organizational behavior* (5th ed.). New York: Wiley.

Trenholm S., & Jenson, V. (1996). *Interpersonal communication* (3rd ed.). New York: Wadsworth.

Weeks, D. (1992). *The eight essential steps to conflict resolution: Preserving relationships at work, at home, and in the community.* New York: Tarcher/Putnam.

Managing Communication Crises

CASE 21
Ethical Issues in Exxon's Response to the Valdez Crisis

CASE 22
Crisis Response: Trans World Airlines and the Crash of TWA Flight 800

CASE 23
Communication Ethics and the Malden Mills Disaster

ETHICAL ISSUES IN EXXON'S RESPONSE TO THE *VALDEZ* CRISIS

Anthony D. McGill and Matthew W. Seeger

When the bottom of the ship *Exxon Valdez* bounced across Bligh Reef at about 12:09 A.M. on March 24, 1989, eight of the tanker's thirteen tanks were ruptured and some of 2.5 million gallons of crude oil began leaking into the pristine waters of Alaska's Prince William Sound. The ship's captain, Joseph Hazelwood, had been notified by the crew moments before that the *Valdez* was in trouble. He came to the bridge and took command from the third mate. Eighteen minutes after the grounding, Hazelwood radioed the Coast Guard in Valdez and asked for help. Officials of Exxon were notified in Houston, Texas, at about 12:30.

Exxon's initial efforts to communicate about the *Valdez* incident were hampered by incomplete information and resources and a decentralized corporate structure. Little information was available about the nature or volume of the spill, and Exxon's corporate public relations offices, located in Texas, initially let local managers handle the crisis. Exxon initially responded to the crisis in a relatively routine manner. The spill itself was characterized as relatively minor, and the company indicated that there was little chance of environmental harm. The press statement released by Exxon and Alyeska on March 24 was also low key:

> The [Valdez] *ruptured several cargo tanks and oil is reported in the water. The amount of the spill is undetermined. An inbound tanker—the Exxon Baton Rouge—has been diverted to the area for possible assistance in off loading the crude oil from the Exxon Valdez if requested by the Coast Guard. The Coast Guard and the Alaska Department of Environmental Conservation are on the scene. Oil Spill cleanup equipment*

is being mobilized at the pipeline terminal and is being dispatched to the scene. [sic] *(Exxon Company USA, March 24, 1989)*

The crisis contingency plan prepared by Alyeska, the consortium that operated the Alaskan Pipeline and Valdez Port, specified that a response team should move immediately to the scene. It was also soon apparent that the specialized equipment needed to respond to the spill was scattered throughout the Valdez Port, disorganized, and in very bad condition. Equipment, including the oil containment boom, was in a warehouse buried under tons of other material. Skimmers to pick up the oil from the surface of the water were not loaded on the spill response barge, and the barge itself was undergoing repairs. The response team, expecting a relatively minor spill, finally left Valdez Harbor ten hours after the grounding and arrived at the spill about fourteen hours after the grounding. (See Figure 21.1.)

When the Alyeska response team finally arrived, it was still not adequately prepared for the spill. Skimmers siphoned oil from the water but had no place to store the reclaimed oil. The containment boom was too light for the choppy open waters of the Sound and for the volume of oil still bleeding from the *Exxon Valdez*. Oil continued to leak from the *Valdez* much faster than it could be contained or reclaimed. Oil spills, by definition, require immediate responses to contain the damage. This failure to respond to the spill in a timely and appropriate manner significantly accelerated the harm.

As it became apparent that mechanical containment and cleanup was inadequate for the volume of oil involved, other options were explored. Exxon officials concluded that the only alternative involved spraying very large quantities of chemical dispersants over the massive slick. Chemical dispersants, agents similar to detergents, break the oil into tiny droplets and allow it to sink to the bottom. These chemical treatments also require some surface wave activity to mix the dispersant with the oil and help break up the slick. Dispersants, although limiting the environmental impact to surface animals, mammals, birds, and beaches, do not remove the spilled oil from the environment. They are generally approved for areas where the environmental impact of the dispersed oil will be minimum. Dispersants are most effective if used before the oil spreads over a wide area.

The long-term environmental impact of dispersants, particularly on sensitive ecosystems, is unknown. Environmentalists see dispersants as cosmetic treatments that remove the oil from view but actually compound the spill with the introduction of additional chemicals. Even though the Alaskan Environmental Agency had approved the area of the *Valdez* grounding for dispersant use, approval was also needed from the

---

FIGURE 21.1   A Chronology of the *Exxon Valdez* Oil Spill

March 24, 1989, 12:09 A.M.
The tanker *Exxon Valdez* grounds on Bligh Reef. Eight of the thirteen tanks are ruptured. The *Valdez* begins to lose about twenty thousand barrels of oil per hour.

March 24, 1989, 12:27 A.M.
Captain Joseph Hazelwood reports the accident to Coast Guard authorities in Valdez Port. The Coast Guard begins the process of notifying various groups.

March 25, 1989, 2:30 P.M.
Alyeska Response Team arrives at the grounded *Valdez* with booms and skimmers. Begins to skim oil and deploy containment boom. Equipment not sufficient to control the volume of oil.

March 28, 1989
A late-winter storm hits Prince William Sound, dispersing the oil over a very wide area and making the use of chemical dispersants ineffective.

March 30, 1989
Exxon announces that Joseph Hazelwood has been fired owing to his violation of company policy with regard to alcohol use.

April 1, 1989
Exxon announces that it was prepared to spray dispersants on the spill on March 25 but did not receive approval from the Coast Guard for three more days.

April 5, 1989
Exxon successfully refloats the damaged tanker *Valdez* after transferring the remaining one million barrels of crude oil to other ships. Attention turns to cleanup.

Coast Guard. Coast Guard officials believed that mechanical retrieval via skimmers should be fully explored before permission was granted and that dispersants initially should only be used in limited tests to assess their effectiveness. This failure to agree among the three major stakeholders— Exxon, the U.S. Coast Guard, and the state of Alaska—created uncertainty and the opportunities for each to shift responsibility.

By the third day, the U.S. Coast Guard granted Exxon permission to use dispersants. It became clear, however, that Exxon only had enough dispersants on site for the treatment of a very small proportion of the spill. Before adequate dispersants could be shipped to the site and applied, a spring storm broke up the slick and spread it over a wide area. The crude oil was now diluted to the point where dispersants would not be nearly as effective or as easily applied.

Exxon's interpretation of these events, however, was that the Coast Guard had needlessly delayed using the most viable option for managing the spill. On April 1, Exxon claimed it had been ready to spray dispersants as early as March 25 but had not received the necessary permission. Lawrence Rawl, Exxon president, later claimed that had the Coast Guard granted permission in a timely fashion, Exxon would have dealt effectively with 50 percent of the oil.

This interpretation served as a preamble to the diffusion of responsibility for the failed cleanup. The Exxon claim was later hotly contested by Coast Guard officials and representatives from the Alaska Department of Environmental Conservation who noted that Exxon had insufficient quantities of chemical dispersants on hand. Governor Steven Cowper of Alaska, in a very strongly worded letter to Rawl dated April 28, 1989, argued "On a number of occasions since the Prince William Sound oil spill, Exxon representatives have claimed that the State of Alaska delayed Exxon's cleanup efforts by refusing to approve the use of chemical dispersants in a timely fashion. Those statements are demonstrably false. Their continued repetition suggests a systematic effort to mislead the public."

Governor Cowper noted that the state was not opposed to the use of dispersants but that the calm sea conditions immediately following the spill did not provide the minimum wave action necessary for dispersants to work effectively in breaking up the oil. Moreover, Cowper noted that dispersants did not remove the oil from the environment and that Exxon did not have sufficient quantities to treat the spill.

Lawrence Rawl responded the same day via facsimile with equally strong portrayals of the cause of the delay:

> *Unfortunately for all concerned, your letter of April 28 does not set the record straight. In fact, it perpetuates a good many wrong assertions. Repetition of incorrect and misleading statements is helpful to no one. We have repeatedly said that immediately after the spill, Exxon requested approval to use chemical dispersants. We have also said that officials of the State of Alaska and the Coast Guard were in discussions during the first three days on whether dispersants should be used. We did not receive the go ahead to use dispersants, other than the two tests, until the end of the three day period ending Sunday evening, March 26th.*

Similar efforts at shifting responsibility occurred when the company identified Captain Joseph Hazelwood as a likely scapegoat for blame and fired him "because he violated Company policy concerning alcohol." Frank Iarossi, president of Exxon Shipping, said, "We are all extremely outraged and disappointed that an officer in such a critical position would jeopardize his ship, crew and the environment through such actions." Hazelwood, who was a natural target for blame due to his position as the captain, became the center of attention as Exxon released additional information about his reported alcoholism.

Initial reports suggested that the accident was caused by a drunken Captain Hazelwood. This interpretation was constructed from reports of (1) Hazelwood drinking while in port, (2) his crew and other officials smelling alcohol on his breath, and (3) empty alcohol containers found in his cabin. Additionally, his blood alcohol level was measured at 0.061 nine hours after the spill. Exxon supported these initial interpretations by firing Hazelwood. Hazelwood was a natural target for blame because as the captain of a ship under way, he was the sole and centralized authority. The popular belief that sea captains have complete authority and control, however, belies the role of the modern captain as subject to the constraints imposed by a complex system of controls. Exxon released additional information about his reported drinking problem, including reports that he had received treatment for alcoholism and that his driver's license had been suspended for drunken driving. These statements served to justify the interpretation of the accident as a consequence of Hazelwood's negligence. Later, Hazelwood's responsibility would be downplayed, and Exxon would admit in testimony before the National Transportation Safety Board that no conclusion could be drawn that Hazelwood was under the influence of alcohol at the time of the accident. The courts and the National Transportation Safety Board would eventually clear Hazelwood of the charge that he was drunk at the time of the accident, making Exxon's earlier interpretations about the cause of the grounding seem both self-serving and deceitful. In still later testimony, however, Hazelwood did admit to having several drinks while in port.

Eventually, the spill cost Exxon billions in compensation paid to the state of Alaska, to fishermen, and for cleanup costs. Important commercial fisheries were closed because of fears of contamination, and thousands of fishermen were idled. Thousands of sea birds became coated in crude oil and died. Their carcasses, along with waves of black crude, washed up on once unspoiled wilderness beaches. Bald eagles, feeding on the carcasses, ingested oil and also died. Many sea otters and other sea mammals also became coated with oil and died. The *Valdez* incident was one the worst environmental incidents ever for the state of Alaska and a public relations disaster for Exxon.

QUESTIONS FOR DISCUSSION

1. What does the *Exxon Valdez* incident suggest about how organizational and individual responsibility should be determined?
2. What can be learned from the *Exxon Valdez* incident about determining how an organization can be held responsible if an employee causes an accident?

3. When an organization creates a harm, what responsibility does the organization have for offsetting the harm? For admitting responsibility? For explaining or justifying procedures and policies?
4. What does the incident help explain about who should serve as spokesperson following an organizational crisis?
5. Some of the "audiences" for Exxon and the state of Alaska are identified in the description of the incident. Are there other important audiences following organizational crises?

SELECTED BIBLIOGRAPHY

Jackall, R. (1988). *Moral mazes—The world of corporate managers*. New York: Oxford University Press.

Perrow, C. (1984). *Normal accidents*. New York: Basic Books.

Petress, K. C., & King, A. (1990). Iran contra and the defeat of accountability. *Communication Reports, 3*, 15–22.

Seeger, M. W. (1997). *Communication, organizing and ethics*. Cresskill, NJ: Hampton.

Williams, D. E., & Treadaway, G. (1992). Exxon and the Valdez accident: A failure in crisis communication. *Communication Studies, 43*(1:), 56–64.

CASE 22

CRISIS RESPONSE

Trans World Airlines and the Crash of TWA Flight 800

Sally J. Ray

BACKGROUND

On the evening of Wednesday, July 17, 1996, Trans World Airlines Flight 800, a Boeing 747, departed New York's JFK International Airport at 8:19 P.M. (EDT). Flight 800, a regularly scheduled flight from New York to Paris, carried 212 passengers and a crew of three pilots and fourteen flight attendants. Approximately fifteen minutes into the flight, TWA 800 crashed into the Atlantic Ocean twenty miles southeast of East Moriches on the eastern end of Long Island. Initial witness reports indicated an explosion and then flaming debris descending to the ocean ("TWA Jetliner," 1996).

Immediately following the crash, the fashionable New York beach resort swarmed with rescue workers, police, and journalists ("TWA Crash," 1996). Wreckage and fuel on the water burned for hours as Coast Guard and Navy planes, along with a small fleet of rescue boats, scoured the dark, choppy waters for signs of life. Scores of volunteers (mariners, fishermen, vacationing boaters) assisted in rescue efforts, pulling human remains from the waters. As darkness fell, parachute flares and floodlights illuminated the waters. The area bordering the crash site was secured. On the beaches fronting the Moriches Inlet, a make-shift morgue was set up. As the night wore on it became evident there were no survivors.

The tragedy brought to an end what otherwise had been a triumphant day. That afternoon, Jeffrey Erickson, president and CEO of Trans World Airlines, in London on a trade mission with officials from Missouri, had announced to reporters in a telephone press conference the airline received a 400 percent gain in its second-quarter earnings. "Our fundamentals are strong and they project to be strong," said Erickson ("Crash Is Latest Blow," 1996).

The St. Louis–based airline, founded by eccentric billionaire Howard Hughes in the 1930s, had reason to celebrate. Deregulation and management upheaval by corporate raider Carl Icahn in the 1980s devastated TWA. In January 1992, the airline filed for Chapter 11 bankruptcy. In November 1993, TWA emerged from bankruptcy with its employees owning 45 percent of the company and creditors owning the remaining 55 percent ("Significant Dates," 1997). In April 1994, Jeffrey Erickson was named president and chief executive officer, and a little over a year later TWA successfully completed a record financial reorganization, placing the airline in its strongest position in ten years.

WEDNESDAY EVENING

In a London hotel, Jeffrey Erickson was in a deep sleep when the phone rang. Joseph Vilmain, TWA's international vice president, was calling with the tragic news. Although Erickson had been in the industry twenty years, he had never been in charge at the time of a major air crash. Mark Abels, TWA's public relations executive, had accompanied Erickson to London. It would be hours before the two would arrive in New York from London.

CRISIS RESPONSE

Throughout the evening, relatives of victims hurried to the TWA terminal at Kennedy in a hysterical quest for information. Learning of the tragedy, Mayor Rudolf Giuliani of New York arrived to assist family members (Firestone, 1996). Although Johanna O'Flaherty, TWA's human resources executive in charge of the trauma team, was vacationing in California, TWA managed to activate its trauma response team and incident coordination center. Responsibilities included notifying next of kin and providing them with information and transportation. In an effort to protect and shield grieving families, the airline gathered victims' families at the Ramada Inn near John F. Kennedy International Airport, providing free lodging, food, and trauma counseling ("Daylight Brings," 1996). Team members assisted families with travel arrangements and necessary paperwork, as well as other needs. Every few hours government officials briefed relatives on the progress of the search.

Media began its coverage shortly after the crash. In St. Louis, Don Monteath, senior vice president of operations, commanded the crisis center. With Erickson and Abels in London, O'Flaherty in California, and the recent resignations of two top executives, few managers were available to respond in New York. In a news conference at JFK Airport, Mike Kelly, TWA staff vice president, issued an official statement. He further commented, "This is the worst possible thing than can happen, and we will attend to it in the best way possible" ("Text of TWA Spokesman Press Conference," 1996).

Reporter: Mr. Kelly, what can family members do if they're watching this right now and have questions?

Kelly: We've set up a place for family members at our terminal five in the Ambassador Club. We have staff over there right now, and we're trying to provide as much service over there as we can for the family members…. They should go there ("Text of TWA Spokesman," 1996).

THURSDAY

The following day, the National Transportation Safety Board's (NTSB) Go-Team, the primary agency in an aviation accident investigation, arrived early and began its investigation. Representatives from Trans World Airlines, Boeing, Pratt & Whitney, the Airline Pilots Association, the Machinist Union, the Federal Aviation Administration, an FBI terrorist team, and the U.S. Bureau of Alcohol, Tobacco, and Firearms were also present at the site.

Obligated to provide information to the public concerning the accident, TWA issued the following statement on its corporate site of the World Wide Web:

Statement Regarding Trans World Airlines Flight 800

July 18, 1996—St. Louis—Trans World Airlines was notified at 8:48 p.m. eastern time on Wednesday July 17 by the FAA that TWA's Flight 800, a 747-100, had left the radar screen approximately 20 miles south of South Hampton in the New York area.

Flight 800 was bound for Paris Charles De Gaulle Airport with 212 passengers and a crew of three pilots and 14 flight attendants. The airline has activated its trauma response team and incident coordination center.

Passengers on Flight 800 were bound for Paris and there were some passengers on board from an earlier canceled flight to Rome.

TWA has established two special numbers for people needing information on Trans World Airline Flight 800, JFK to Paris, July 17: 1-800-438-9892 or 1-800-819-5321. These numbers are intended for relative inquiries only.

TWA is deeply concerned for the safety of its passengers and crew and is working closely with federal and local officials. TWA will not make further comment until information can be verified. ("Statement Regarding," 1996)

That afternoon, Erickson and Abels arrived from London. Rumors concerning a bomb had spread rapidly since the explosion appeared too violent for a mechanical malfunction ("No evidence," 1996). At a New York press conference Abels indicated there was no suggestion of a threat to the aircraft. He commented, "It is our understanding from the various traffic control centers and centers that were in radio contact with the flight, that there were no non-routine transmissions from the flight whatsoever, and no indication of any problem until the flight disappeared and went silent" ("TWA 800 Crash," 1996).

Initially, there was confusion as to the number of passengers on board. According to Abels, the flight carried 228 people, citing 210 passengers and 18 crew members. Earlier reports of 229 had been incorrect. (The actual count was 230.) At that time, 140 bodies had been recovered. Abels indicated thirty-five passengers were TWA flight personnel on their way to assignment in Europe. TWA president and CEO Jeffrey Erickson stated, "Our task now is to honor the memory of our lost colleagues by caring for the families and each other" ("TWA 800 Crash," 1996).

PUBLIC RESPONSE

The crash of TWA Flight 800 occurred during a period of increased anxiety over both airline safety and terrorist attacks. In April, an Air Force plane carrying Secretary of Commerce Ron Brown and others crashed, killing all on board. The following month, a ValuJet commercial aircraft crashed in the Florida Everglades, killing 110 passengers. The fact that this latest crash happened in New York, media capitol of the world, increased media coverage. There was great public concern and interest. The *New York Times'* "CyberTimes" reported the crash prompted a record turnout of computer users on the World Wide Web, in search for information about the crash (Barboza, 1996). Web sites devoted to the crash were established by major news organizations, as well as individuals.

Throughout the day, TWA received a barrage of criticism from Mayor Giuliani and victims' relatives for failing to promptly complete a formal passenger list and notify relatives. Frank Capuzzo, a friend of one victim stated, "I think there are two tragedies here—the tragedy that of course, occurred last night, but even a greater tragedy is the way we, the families, have been treated by TWA.... It is now 15 or 16 hours after the crash, and to the best of my knowledge, TWA still has not contacted the parents of that child in France" ("TWA 800 Crash," 1996).

Mayor Giuliani publicly criticized TWA management for its inadequate response. Criticism concerned the absence of high-ranking TWA officials and the airline's delay in confirming the passenger list. The airline's response that the NTSB was the source for delay was vehemently denied by the NTSB. That evening on *Larry King Live,* guests included the mayor and New York's Governor Pataki. Both continued their attack on the airline.

King: What—what were you angry or are you angry at?

Giuliani: I was quite disturbed that they didn't produce the list from which you could verify the people on this flight, until about 4:00 this afternoon and that is just unacceptable. That should have been done sometime last night. Families are going through enough heartbreak and enough fear and worry; we can't remove that for them, but we can make things easier for them, not harder for them. There were a lot of very good people from TWA working with the families, working with the people that were concerned, but at the upper management level they were nonexistent at Kennedy Airport.

King: Governor Pataki, do you share that criticism?

Pataki: I do. It was incomprehensible to me that more than 12 hours after the catastrophe, people still couldn't get an answer as to whether their son or parent was in fact on the plane. And a lot has been straightened out since but certainly there was a lot more that I believe could have been done sooner on behalf of the families" ("TWA Flight 800," 1996).

FRIDAY

Receiving national attention, Giuliani kept up his disapproval for the second day. On Friday, the mayor reported to CNN he'd been lied to by TWA.

Reporter: Mr. Mayor, is there going to be more of an effort now because of what happened, to shift notification from airlines to government agency?

Giuliani: The legislation…was handed to me this morning when I was on television. I have not had a chance to read it…. There's no question that the way TWA handled it—this could be improved significantly.

Reporter: Do you think you were too hard on them initially?

Giuliani: No, I think I was too easy on them.

Reporter: Mayor, are you satisfied with the actions taken by TWA?

Giuliani: I think they're doing what they can to help the families. I don't think they've adequately disclosed the facts of what led up to it, and I continue to hear them saying things that are not true, which always disturbs me when people do that. I mean the fact is that I was directly told by the President of TWA that the NTSB prohibited them from handing out the list. I talked to the chairman of the NTSB and the vice-chairman, directly, on the telephone one person-to-person, who tell me that this is totally false. This morning I listened to a representative of TWA say that all the families were notified by noon yesterday. That's totally false. They hadn't even compiled a list by noon yesterday. When I left here with the governor, they still hadn't compiled the list. When I got back here at four o'clock, they were still working on it. So my response to it is, a very, very good practice to follow, in government or in corporate communications is, tell the truth. ("Text of Giuliani's," 1996)

TWA RESPONDS

In response to the criticism, TWA officials contended that they had acted responsibly (Meier, 1996). The TWA spokesman, Mark Abels, acknowledged the mayor's disappointment, agreeing the process should be quicker, but emphasized the need for accuracy. Erickson expressed his appreciation to the mayor and his trauma response team which supplemented the airline's efforts. Although it was some twenty-four hours after the crash before TWA's crisis team was in place, Erickson stated the airline's trauma response team's efforts were now full scale.

That evening TWA's director of media relations, John McDonald, defended the airline's actions following the crash in a CNN interview:

[I]t's very unfortunate that the focus has been dropped from the families involved and from the accident investigation into some sort of a "who knew what when" routine. We have an obligation to notify the family as soon as we have an ability to do that, and we, as has been mentioned before, were determined to do it right. And sometimes we'll have to take heat because of that, because we don't do it as quickly as everyone would like to have it.... It is not as simple as some have said.... There are a number of resources that we have to compile and then collate and start working through it, reservation and person by person, to try and verify it. And if all the pieces don't fit, there's some problem, then we have to determine whether or not this is accurate, and that is a painstaking process. And when you're talking about more than 200 people, it just isn't as easy and as quick as people would like.

When asked about the mayor's relentless criticism of the airline, Mc-Donald stated:

> I can't comment on why the Mayor is doing what he's doing, and it's not my intent. My intent is to let people know that TWA has spared no expense and has spared no effort on personnel and time to make sure that this list was compiled as quickly as possible. TWA lost more than 50 of its own family on that airplane, and it is very unfair, I think to say somehow that TWA was not in any way interested in making sure that these people were told as quickly as possible.

Responding to whether TWA would reconsider its policies for handling these crises, McDonald stated:

> One of the things that is done in any accident is that you have a debriefing after everything is done. So we definitely will review all of our policies and procedures after this incident is over and the investigation is well under way, to see what we can do better on all fronts. ("TWA Spokesman Defends" 1996)

QUESTIONS FOR DISCUSSION

1. Describe how you think TWA responded following the crash? What complicated the airline's response efforts?
2. What did TWA do to reassure the public and demonstrate concern and compassion?
3. Why was TWA criticized for its response to the crash? What were the major issues?
4. How did TWA respond to Mayor Giuliani's criticism?
5. What should TWA have done to improve its response following the crash? What variables should TWA have factored into its crisis plan?
6. What does this case suggest about the utility of the World Wide Web as a means for communicating during crisis?

REFERENCES

Barboza, D. (1996, August 5). After the TWA crash, the web proves its worth is headline service and bulletin board. *New York Times CyberTimes*. [On-line]. No longer available.

Crash is latest blow to TWA. (1996, July 18). *CNN Interactive* [On-line]. Available: http://cnnfn.com/hotstor...es/9607/18/twa-business/

Daylight brings no trace of survivors of TWA crash. (1996, July18). *CNN Interactive* [On-line]. Available: http://www.cnn.com/us/9607/18/twa.7a/index.html

Firestone, D. (1996, July 20). Politicians provide comfort and criticism after crash. *New York Times.*

Meier, B. (1996, July 23). TWA's Erickson trying to give answers when there aren't any. *New York Times* [On-line]. Available: http://www.nytimes.com/y...t/twa-crash-airline.html/

Significant dates in TWA history. (1997, October 12). *Trans World Airlines* [On-line]. Available: http://www.twa.com/html/contact/sigdates.html

Statement regarding Trans World Airlines Flight 800. (1996, July 18). *Trans World Airlines* [On-line]. Available: http://www.twa.com/

Text of Giuliani's Flight 800 briefing—Part 1. (1996, July 19). *CNN Specials,* Transcript #849.

Text of TWA spokesman press conference on Flight 800. (1996, July 17). *CNN Breaking News.* Broadcast News ™, Vol. BN199607 Transcript, p. 1.

TWA 800 crash—Victims being comforted. (1996, July 18). *CNN Specials.* Transcript #848.

TWA crash transforms Long Island resort. (1996, July 18). *CNN Interactive* [On-line]. Available: http://www.cnn.com/us/96...twa.scene.wir/index.html

TWA Flight 800. (1996, July 18). *Larry King Live.* Transcript #1803.

TWA jetliner leaving New York for Paris crashes in Atlantic. (1996, July 18). *New York Times* p. A1.

TWA spokesman defends airline's actions since crash. (1996, July 19). *Early Prime* (CNN). Transcript #1291, Segment 1.

SELECTED BIBLIOGRAPHY

Fink, S. (1986). *Crisis management: Planning for the inevitable.* New York: AMACOM.

Milburn, T. W., Schuler, R. S., & Watman, K. H. (1983). Organizational crisis. Part I: definition and conceptualization. *Human Relations, 36,* 1141–1160.

Milburn, T. W., Schuler, R. S., & Watman, K. H. (1983). Organizational crisis. Part II: strategies and responses. *Human Relations, 36,* 1161–1180.

Pinsdorf, M. K. (1987). *Communicating when your company is under seige: Surviving public crisis.* Lexington, MA: Lexington.

COMMUNICATION ETHICS AND THE MALDEN MILLS DISASTER
Robert R. Ulmer and Matthew W. Seeger

Malden Mills, located in Lawrence, Massachusetts, is a company with a strong history of social responsibility. It is one of the region's largest employers and is one of the few textile businesses still located in the northeast. The mill produces the registered trademark fabrics of Polartech, Polarfleece, Boundary, and Glenn Street. Malden Mills is one of the two largest fabric mills in the United States, producing about 750,000 yards out of an industry total of two million. Most other textile companies in the area fled to escape the high prices for energy and the 20 percent higher wages the strong unions of the area demand.

Aaron Feuerstein, the owner of Malden Mills, consistently refused to move, contending the workers' technical skills outweighed the benefits of moving to a location with cheaper labor costs. Paul Coorey, president of the Union of Needleworkers, Industrial and Textile Employees, explained that Feuerstein is "a man of his word." Ronald Alman, the chief of the New England union, remarked, "He's extremely compassionate for people." Moreover, Feuerstein "believes in the process of collective bargaining and he believes that if you pay people a fair amount of money, and give them good benefits to take care of their families, they will produce for you." In an era when organizations increasingly stress profits through downsizing and streamlining strategies, this level of employer loyalty is uncommon. Feuerstein places value for employees as an integral component of organizational success (Nyhan, 1995).

On December, 11, 1995, Aaron Feuerstein's seventieth birthday, a devastating explosion destroyed three of his textile mills, resulting in thirty-six injuries, eight of which were critical. The *Boston Globe* characterized the event by stating, "After the initial blast, a series of smaller explosions continued to rock the complex for hours. Just before midnight, an explosion sent a charcoal-colored cloud of chemicals soaring into the sky" (Butterfield, 1996). Throughout the evening of the explosion, the flames surged fifty feet into the sky. The intensity of the blaze forced local residents surrounding the mill to evacuate.

As a result of the explosion and subsequent fire, 1,400 employees faced layoffs two weeks before Christmas. The next day, December 12, with his mill still burning behind him, Feuerstein vowed to rebuild rather than taking the insurance money and moving the mill. He stated, "We had the opportunity to run to the South many years ago. We didn't do it then, and we're not going to do it now" (Milne and Aucoin, 1995). One day later, on December 13, employees were surprised when they came to pick up what they thought would be their final paychecks. Feuerstein not only had their checks waiting, but he also provided the $275 holiday bonus he promised before the fire. In addition, employees were given gift certificates to a local supermarket (Milne, 1995). Workers were also asked to attend a meeting the next day, December 14, to learn about their employment future.

On December 14, 1995, at a local high school, over one thousand of the mill's workers sat eagerly awaiting Feuerstein's remarks. He stated that "at least for the next thirty days—the time might be longer—all our hourly employees will be paid their full salaries." Health insurance will be covered for the next ninety days. Employees erupted into a standing ovation. By the end of the meeting Feuerstein was mobbed by employees expressing their gratitude (Milne, 1995).

On December 23, 1995, less than two weeks after the fire, employees received more good news: Malden Mills was resuming partial production of their operations, allowing three hundred employees to return to work ("Damaged mill," 1995). By January 11, 1996, 65 percent of the mill employees were back at work. However, January 11 was the one-month anniversary of the fire and the end of Feuerstein's original agreement with workers to pay full salaries for thirty days. For unemployed workers as of January 11, Feuerstein held another meeting to address the needs of these employees.

At the January 11 meeting, Feuerstein informed workers that he would pay salaries for a second thirty-day period. The announcement produced a roar of applause and shouts from the crowd of workers. Above the cheers, a reporter for The *Boston Globe* heard one worker shout "God Bless you, Aaron." Another proclaimed, "This has got to be the best company in America." Feuerstein responded to worker gratitude by stating, "I consider the employees standing in front of me here the most valuable asset that Malden Mills has. I don't consider them, like some companies do, as an expense that can be cut" ("Workers praise," 1996). Feuerstein expected that most of his employees would be back to work in thirty to ninety days and some would be recalled earlier. However, the flock division of the company, which was hardest hit by the fire, would take a year to recover.

Through Feuerstein's response to an organizational disaster he was able to create a positive impact both on the organization and the community. Interestingly, when asked about his response to the crisis, Feuerstein stated, "I know that in the long run that what I'm doing today will come back tenfold and will make Malden Mills the best company in the industry" ("Methuen's good," 1995).

QUESTIONS FOR DISCUSSION

1. What communication strategies can help build trust among the constituencies before a crisis?
2. What responsibilities does an organization have to employees following a crisis?
3. What aspects of Feuerstein's response might be considered examples of ethical communication?
4. What outcomes would you expect as a consequence of Feuerstein's response?

REFERENCES

Butterfield, B. D. (1996, September 9). Nobody burned down Malden Mills. *The Boston Globe*, p. A17.

Damaged mill starts work. (1995, December 23). *The New York Times*, p. A6.

Methuen's good fortune. (1995, December 16). *The Boston Globe*, p. A14.

Milne, J. (1995, December 14). Mill owner pledges limited reopening soon; company pays bonuses; offers of relief widen. *The Boston Globe*, p. A43.

Milne, J. (1995, December 15). Mill owner says he'll pay workers for a month. *The Boston Globe*, p. B50.

Milne, J., & Aucoin, D. (1995, December 13, 1995). In flicker of flames, mill owner vows to rebuild. *The Boston Globe*, p. B1.

Nyhan, D. (1995, December 17). The mensch who saved Christmas. *The Boston Globe*, p. A20.

Workers praise boss for extending benefits after fire destroyed mill. (1996, January 12). *The Chicago Tribune*, p. 2C.

SELECTED BIBLIOGRAPHY

Freeman, R. E. (1984). *Strategic management: A stakeholder approach.* Marshfield, MA: Pitman.

Herrick, J. A. (1992). Rhetoric, ethics and virtue. *Communication Studies, 43,* 133–150.

Prince, S. H. (1920). *Catastrophe and social change.* New York: Columbia University Press.

Seeger, M. W., & Bolz, B. (1996). Technological transfer and multinational corporations in the Union Carbide crisis in Bhopal, India. In J. A. Jaksa & M. S. Pritchard (Eds.), *Responsible communication: Ethical issues in business, industry, and the professions* (pp. 245–265). Cresskill, NJ: Hampton.

Sellnow, T. L., & Ulmer, R. R. (1995). Ambiguous argument as advocacy in organizational crisis communication. *Argumentation and Advocacy, 31*, 138–150.

APPENDIX

ABOUT THE AUTHORS

Andrews, Paul. B.A., Union College (Schenectady, NY). He is a PC columnist and hi-tech reporter for the *Seattle Times,* the largest daily newspaper in Seattle, Washington. He continues to write extensively about Microsoft and has published a book about Microsoft's founder: *Gates: How Microsoft's Mogul Reinvented the Industry and Made Himself the Richest Man in America* (Doubleday, 1993).

Burke, Beverly C. B.A., psychology, St. Cloud State University; M.S., health services administration, Cardinal Stritch College. She is currently an RN on the Mental Health Unit (MHU) of Rice Memorial Hospital, Willmar, MN.

Cavenagh, Thomas D. J.D., DePaul University College of Law. His experience is with law and conflict resolution.

Fearon, Robyn. She is a former director of the Leadership Forum in Singapore and a consultant to major international companies.

Gayle, Barbara Mae. M.A., University of Portland; Ph.D., University of Oregon. She is a professor and chair of the Communication Studies Department, University of Portland (OR). In addition to teaching organizational communication, communication research methods, and negotiation and conflict management, she has published articles in *Management Communication Quarterly, Women's Studies in Communication, Journal of Applied Communication Research,* and *Journal of Communication Research Reports.*

Gregg, Nina. M.A., Ph.D., McGill University. She is founder/consultant of Communication Resources and has done consulting since 1992 in not-for-profit and for-profit sectors on participatory work processes and organizational change. Her recent publications include articles in *At Work* and *Women's Studies in Communication.*

Hammond, Scott. M.A., organizational behavior, Brigham Young University; Ph.D., University of Utah. He is an assistant professor of communications at Brigham Young. Consultant in globalization and cross-cultural issues for scientific and technical organizations.

Jaeger, Deborah. M.A., University of Southern California. She is a marketing professional managing projects in France, Belgium, Italy, and Eastern Europe.

Kincaid, Diana Woods. Ph.D., Northwestern University. Her work is in communication, gender and law.

*Locklear, Regina. B.A., communication, University of Puget Sound. She has experience as a quality circles facilitator, as a human resource development specialist for management and supervisory development programs for a state government agency, and a project specialist for a major state agency.

McGill, Anthony. M.A., Michigan University; Ph.D., Wayne State University. Assistant professor in the Communication Department at the University of Michigan–Flint. He is involved in numerous consulting activities and serves on the board of directors/public relations manager, Oakbrook Table Tennis Training Facility.

*McNutt, Tom. B.A., University of Puget Sound. He is field training manager for Japan, Pacific Rim, and Latin America for high-technology companies in the United States. He also has trained in selling skills programs on several continents and in over a dozen countries.

Merritt, Martha M. B.A., M.A.T. in business education; master's of accountancy, University of South Carolina; CPA. She is an assistant professor of accounting, Department of Business Administration, North Georgia College.

Morris, David E., Sr. B.S.B.A., accounting; master's of accountancy; Ph.D, accounting; CPA. He is an assistant professor of accounting, North Georgia College, and has published in both academic and professional journals; he is also a member of the American Institute of CPAs.

Peterson, Gary L. M.A., Ph.D., Ohio University. He is emeritus professor of communication, University of Puget Sound. In addition to serving as editor and compiler of this casebook and *Instructor's Guide,* he has nearly twenty-five years of teaching experience in organizational communication. He also is a consultant in employee communication and organizational analysis for public and private firms.

---

*Names of these authors have been changed to protect individual identities.

Pierson, Jillian K. Ph.D., University of Southern California. She serves as lecturer in communication at the Annenberg School of Communication at the University of Southern California, where she teaches organizational communication and intercultural communication. Her primary research interest is communication in multinational organizations. Her doctoral dissertation is a dialectical approach to understanding the dynamics of cultural interactions among members of global work teams.

Rauschenberg, Gretchen. M.A., University of Illinois; Ph.D., Ohio University. In the organization described in the case, she was in her second year of a three- to five-year longitudinal study of organizational communication within one district and branch offices. She has served as a consultant/ trainer in communication needs assessments and training programs.

Ray, Sally J. Ph.D., Wayne State University. She is an associate professor of communication at Western Kentucky University. Her research on crisis communication in the airline industry has spanned almost a decade. Her book, *Strategic Communication in Crisis Management: Lessons from the Airline Industry,* is expected for publication in the spring of 1999. Dr. Ray teaches graduate and undergraduate courses in crisis communication, organizational communication, and interpersonal communication.

Ringer, R. Jeffrey. Ph.D., Ohio University. He is a communication professor at St. Cloud State University (MN).

Schillar, Thomas E. M.A., Eastern Washington University; Ph.D., Colorado State University. He is the director of the Small Business Institute, University of Puget Sound. As a consultant and trainer, he had direct experience with the organization described in case eighteen.

Seeger, Matthew W. Ph.D., Indiana University. He is an associate professor in the Department of Communication and assistant dean of the Graduate School. His teaching and research in organizational communication, communication ethics, and crisis and issue management are nationally recognized. His edited book *"I Gotta Tell You:" Speeches of Lee Iacocca* (Wayne State University Press, 1994), is a resource for students of organizational communication, leadership, and corporate advocacy. His second book, *Ethics in Organizational Communication* (Hampton, 1997), reviews the range of ethical issues associated with organizational communication.

Shapiro, Elayne J. M.A.; Ph.D., University of Minnesota. She is an assistant professor of communication studies at the University of Portland (OR). In addition to teaching organizational communication, interpersonal communication, and leadership, she has consulting experience with banks, hospitals, and unions. Recent research examines personal Web pages and conflict on E-mail.

Singleton, Tim. He is the Lee Anderson Professor of Management, North Georgia College and State University; Fulbright Scholar Exchange to Bulgaria in 1997–1998. He has served on the *Case Research Journal* editorial board from 1985 to the present, published thirty-five cases in ninety texts and journals, and was a North American Case Research Association Fellow in 1998.

Tubbs, Stewart L. M.A., Bowling Green State University; Ph.D., University of Kansas, with postdoctoral study at Harvard Business School. He is the dean of the College of Business, Eastern Michigan University. He has consulted for more than one hundred organizations, mostly Fortune 500 companies. He has chaired the Organizational Communication Division of the Academy of Management and has numerous publications in interpersonal communication, human communication, and group decision making.

Ulmer, Robert R. Ph.D. Wayne State University. He is an assistant professor of speech communication at the University of Arkansas at Little Rock. His work has appeared in *Communication Yearbook 21* and the *North Dakota Journal of Speech and Theatre.* His articles are forthcoming in *Communication Studies* and *Communication Quarterly.*

Vincent, Roger. Ph.D. Ohio State University. He is a team leader, human resources and organizational development, for ARCO/Alcan. He has served also as organizational development specialist and director of training in other firms.

Welsh, Michael F. He is an associate professor of higher education in the Department of Educational Leadership and Policies at the University of South Carolina. He is a member of the Southeastern Case Research Association, and the North American Case Research Association. His case, *Columbia College and Leadership for Women,* was just published in Jeffrey Harrison and Caron St. John's text, *Strategic Management of Organizations and Stakeholders* (West, 1993). In addition to his research in South Africa, he has presented workshops to university faculty groups on researching, writing and using case studies in college courses.